COME AUTUMN, *Memoirs* OF A HUNTER

DON DANIELSON

authorHOUSE®

AuthorHouse™
1663 Liberty Drive
Bloomington, IN 47403
www.authorhouse.com
Phone: 1 (800) 839-8640

Published by AuthorHouse 07/24/2019

ISBN: 978-1-7283-2064-9 (sc)
ISBN: 978-1-7283-2053-3 (hc)
ISBN: 978-1-7283-2065-6 (e)

Print information available on the last page.

This book is printed on acid-free paper.

Lovingly Dedicated to Lady Phyllis

COME AUTUMN!

Throbbing drums and furtive shadows no longer were sounded or sighted along the shores of Mirror Lake. Nevertheless, mental images of Native Americans dashed in my eight-year old mind and were kept alive by books, stories, and periodic visits to burial sites and effigy mounds near home. Home was Waupaca, said by many residents to mean 'tomorrow' in Indian. Others say the town's name comes from Chief Wapuka (Wa-pukka) who lived in the area.

Exploding out the front door right after lunch from our new house, my Mom called out, "Remember Donny, Papa is home so be back for supper at six o'clock!" Indeed, 'Papa is home'! He is home after spending almost five years in the South Pacific, mainly New Guinea, Australia, and the Philippine Islands during WWII. My sister Deanne was born shortly after Papa left for the war. At that time, I was almost three years old. We watched him board the Soo Line train at our little city depot. That was in 1940. He and about a hundred other National Guardsmen went off to WWII with the 32nd Division, 127th Battalion from Waupaca, WI.

Now we were together, a complete, happy family! Mom and Pop just bought a house on Mirror Lake about five blocks from downtown. New surroundings fire-up innumerable interests and possibilities for a little inquisitive guy like me. Long-standing inquisitiveness can be documented. In my 1955 High School Yearbook, under my graduation picture is the comment "He would stop St. Peter's roll call to ask a question."

At the time, I thought about the Indians who first traipsed the shoreline, caught the fish and game and who built the Indian mounds. And I thought about the first settlers. I knew a little bit about the pioneers who homesteaded or settled our town, cleared the land, built the houses and farms. My great grandfather was one of them. Already, at the age of eight I started to appreciate those who came before us and lived where we live before it became "our turn."

It was a big new world to me, composed of innumerable little worlds.

Our backyard ended at the lake. What a great place to grow up, to start exploring. Whole new natural worlds were opening up. And it was summertime! Frogs and fish, damselflies and dragonflies. Trees and bushes, birds and animals. I opened decaying logs and looked for grubs and ants; overturned rocks to see 'pedes scurrying from light. Life in many forms scampered and scrambled for life. It became obvious: nature often provided to each square foot a generous supply of creatures, living and competing and cooperating in innumerable little worlds of their own. Right in our own backyard! It was soul stirring! Exciting to the marrow of my bones!

"Butch" also lived on Mirror Lake, up around the corner on Main Street. Our yards met at right angles. Butch became my best friend throughout grade, junior high, high school and into old age. His dad was one of two doctors in town. Dr. Boudry introduced his whole family -- wife, two daughters and two sons -- to the sports of hunting and fishing. They even had a shooting range in their basement, which I thought was about the neatest thing a house could have! "Butch" was the youngest of their family and three years older than me. I looked up to Butch. We became inseparable friends, but it didn't start out that way.

Eager to scope-out my new environs, probably a day or so after we moved into our new house, after a quick lunch I started up Lake Street when Mom said be home for supper by six o'clock. Then I turned toward South Park at the end of Main Street. I stopped to visit another boy on the way named Billy who said I could climb the tall White Spruce tree in his front yard with him. That's when Butch and I first met. He lived next door to Billy.

Butch's family was just returning from vacation and evidently Butch saw me from their car as they were coming down Main Street. He came boiling out of their car, wanting to know what I was doing in <u>his</u> tree. After I smugly pointed out where he lived, and where Billy lived, and where the tree was located, Butch beat the snot out of me for my insolence. Blood sealed our friendship. Mostly mine. Following this introduction, our friendship spanned six decades.

The shore of Mirror Lake was an ideal place to grow up. How I loved Mirror Lake! Although small (less than a mile long and half as wide), it was deep. Mirror Lake was connected by a hundred-yard long, twenty-foot wide channel to Shadow Lake and the city's South Shore Park and Beach. Shadow Lake was larger than Mirror and also the lake where Butch and I shot our first Snow Goose, which had mostly swan-like characteristics. Mirror Lake contained mostly panfish and bass, but Butch's father, Dr. Boudry caught some trout in the deep-water end of the lake on a rig he trolled behind his boat called a "cow bell" -- about seven or eight spinners in line, and on the end was a lure. Lucky for us, the Boudry's had a dock and often up to six boys would be fishing from their dock. "Shooter Bill" who worked for Remington Arms and Dr. Remmel who was the town dentist had the other two docks on the lake, but their docks were not where the fishing was best. Dr. Boudry put some large, log "fish cribs" that he built out on the ice about twenty-five feet from their dock. The crib was made of logs which were wired together and then weighted with concrete blocks. In Spring when the ice melted, the cribs sunk and settled where he wanted them and the fishing became the best around the cribs – but you had to know exactly where the logs were or you would lose a lure.

During our grade school years in the spring, summer, and fall, I often camped overnight in our backyard. I pretended that I was an Indian, or mountain man, or bushwacker, or mule skinner, or army scout, or bounty hunter, or hunting guide, or fishing guide – according to my whims. Almost always I camped alone in our backyard. The calls of owls, loons, soras, bitterns, coots and other waterbirds, especially at night, were both alluring and intriguing!

Since Papa stayed in the U. S. Army National Guard when he came home from the war, he was able to get me an Army pup tent and an Army sleeping bag. Pup tents are intended to be used in tandem with another pup tent. They buttoned together, end-to-end, to accommodate two soldiers. The "outside" unbuttoned ends of the joined tents were slanted out and staked to the ground. This slanted "pocket" at both ends of the joined tents was used for storage for each of the two occupants. Since I had just one part of a two-man tent, I slept with my head in the "pocket." Sometimes when I was not intending to sleep out, I checked the weather report and changed my mind if rain was predicted. I loved sleeping out when it rained.

Today's light-weight, down-filled, rip-stop, wind breaking, zippered, insulated "guaranteed-to-ten-below-zero" tents hardly compare to the WWII sleeping bag I had, and that American soldiers all over the world used. The army sleeping bag was three single-bed widths of canvas sewn together side-by-side. The middle piece of canvas was the heaviest because it was the part of the sleeping bag in contact with the ground. The other two "flaps" of canvas on each side folded alternately over the bottom canvas. I put folded blankets inside this ensemble which was then fastened together by three canvas straps. It was a heavy canvas sleeping bag and some nights two or three blankets were required to keep warm. Seldom, without clothespins pinning the blankets together, would the blankets stay together all night. Nevertheless, I was very attached to my tent and sleeping bag. It was fun to push off from shore in our old rowboat just before daybreak after building a small campfire, catch a couple bluegills and return to my campsite for a breakfast of fried fresh fish. Not wanting to arouse the family that early in the morning by going up to the house and getting a frying pan, the first time I caught a couple bluegills for breakfast I fried them on a shovel. At the bottom of our backyard, past the huge oak tree near the fence at the property line, I dug worms. On that very "milestone morning" I cleaned the shovel with sand and water at the shore, heated it over the coals of my little campfire to kill the germs, and put the cleaned fish on the shovel. Later, when I was in the Boy Scouts, I had a real cook kit. The shovel worked fairly well, except the fish skin stuck to the shovel. No big deal. The flaky, white meat was so hot and delicious! With a pinch of salt, the flavor would have been even better.

Butch, Jerry, and Bill had bamboo flyrods, but mine was steel and telescoped. Steel fly rods were cheap and heavy. My right arm was often tired by noon. This was specially so during early June when I would climb a willow tree down at the shore and shimmy out on a limb over the water. I would dangle worms over the spawning bluegills and sunfish in their nests directly below. It was so easy to catch spawning fish – peering directly down on their spawning beds from about twenty feet above them. I could drop a worm right in front of the fish's nose! Even rub their snout with the worm! Near as I could figure, the fish struck the

bait for one of two reasons – either it was hungry or it was mad and going to drive the intruding worm from its nest. Our family ate lots of fish. Back then, I scaled and eviscerated the fish. We ate the crunchy fins. Learning to filet a fish came later for me when I caught bigger fish.

Butch's family had a small pond in their backyard that was connected to the lake with a five-foot wide channel about thirty feet long. For a few years they raised ducks in the pond. Their wing-clipped, domestic ducks attracted wild ducks, **come autumn**. Although hunting was not permitted inside the city limits where we lived, during the waterfowl season Butch and I pinged a couple ducks with our .22s on Mirror Lake. This was not a very safe practice because the bullets could skip off the water. We also hunted rabbits, mostly across the lake along the shore where two elderly, single ladies who were teachers lived. The two beagles the Boudrys owned were named Spic and Span. When those dogs flushed a bunny and started baying, all you had to do is turn around and wait. The dogs would usually bring the bunny right around to you in less than a minute. For one reason, the lake hemmed them in on one side. For another reason, up on the high ground fifty yards from the lake, the brush along the shore gave way to lawns and houses where there was little to no cover. The two eighth grade teachers, Mesdames McGregor and Rhinehart, knew it was Butch and me shooting the rabbits. For some reason, they never said anything to either one of us in person or at school when they saw us – but they did yell at us from their back door when they heard a shot! When they yelled, they used our names!

On the same east side of Mirror Lake was a huge ice house. The ice was usually cut after a long freeze. On another part of the lake, the City would plow a quarter mile oval for skaters and we would ice-skate and play hockey almost every day of the two weeks of Christmas Vacation, except of course where the ice had been cut. I still have a scar on my throat from being goalie with a scoop snow shovel. Blocking a shot on goal, the shovel scooped the puck up and into my throat. I walked the four blocks to the hospital for stitches, leaving a trail of blood, of which I was very proud and showed my sister. We soaked cattail seed heads in kerosene during the day and lighted them for torches when we skated at night.

Mirror Lake played a big part in our youth when growing up. With safe ice and little snow, we would sometimes even skate through the channel and into Shadow Lake. Ice-fishing was quite popular on Mirror Lake and it was unusually exciting when a car went through the ice!

To get the car out, a four-sided "crib" was made from huge, alternately stacked timbers to about ten feet high on top of the ice so the submerged vehicle could be winched off the bottom of the lake set down on cross beams that spanned the hole. The car was then pulled off the lake for drying out.

In the summer, although it was forbidden and so said the "No Trespassing" signs on the big ice house building, we made forts in the ice house. We even rearranged some of the blocks to make caves. Cool. In the summertime, very cool! The few families who still had ice boxes in town instead of refrigerators which were becoming more and more popular, put their "ice signs" in their front window on "ice days" which was usually twice a week. If the sign had the "25" right side up and the "50" upside down on the bottom, the occupants wanted 25 pounds of ice that day. On hot summer days, we would walk behind the delivery horse and wagon, later an open-bed truck with a heavy tarpaulin covering the ice. If the iceman had to chisel a fifty-pound block of ice into two twenty-five pound blocks, ice chips would fall on the road and the fastest kid would get the biggest chunk of ice! We also dug warm, black tar out of the cracks in the streets and chewed it like gum.

By the time I was twelve, I already had a bolt action, five shot clip .22, mostly for squirrels and rabbits. I cannot remember exactly how I got the .22, but a  Christmas picture of my sister and me when we were about nine and twelve respectively, shows me in my pajamas in front of the Christmas tree aiming the rifle. Butch had a shotgun. I really wanted a shotgun which meant I could hunt ducks, geese, and maybe even deer, besides squirrels and rabbits.

I probably whined about getting a shotgun and one afternoon, after Pop finished his rural mail route of fifty miles and with about one hundred and fifty farm mailboxes, you could've bowled me over with a feather!

Papa bought a vintage .410 shotgun from Floyd who was the sheriff of Waupaca County! We paid $8 for it. I say "we" because Papa paid half and I paid half. It was a single shot (break at the breech), with a thumb hammer, small bore, marvelous work of art! I re-blued the barrel and varnished the stock and forearm. Floyd and Arlene and my folks were very close friends. I was named after their older son Donald. My first "hunt" with a shotgun was when Papa took me out on his mail route – I think the next day – where he had frequently seen crows. I remember shooting but I don't remember hitting anything except stationary targets that helped me understand the difference between a rifle with one projectile and a shotgun that had many pellets as multiple projectiles. Hence the phrase, "Aim the rifle, point the shotgun." Pop was not a hunter after he came back from the war. Nevertheless, I was very thankful for the .410 and thankful to Papa taking me out for some hunter safety instructions.

Butch and I hunted squirrels most weekends and often after school. One "bluebird Saturday," Butch said his dad would take us duck hunting that afternoon! My very first duck hunt! One of Dr. Boudry's patients had a farm pond out toward Ogdensburg that had some locally hatched, wild puddle ducks on it. Mostly mallards and teal. It was a pleasant, sunny, warm Saturday afternoon. A day more suited to picnicking than duck hunting. But these were local ducks, hatched, raised, and at home on the pond. Weather was the least of my concerns. I was going duck hunting with Butch and his father! With shotguns! Butch had a pump Remington 870 "Wingmaster" twelve gauge, plugged, and I had my single-shot .410.

I remember having a couple live shells clamped between my fingers in case I needed to quickly reload. Dr. Boudry deployed the three of us and we were probably a hundred yards apart, triangulating the small pond of approximately two or three acres. After getting secured and pulling cattails and bulrushes down around us, Dr. Boudry yelled, "Donny, behind you!" About eight

Blue-Winged Teal were hurtling down from the sky toward the pond. Turning around, I crumpled the first one of the flock. It bounced once when it hit the water because it was going so fast. Quickly reloading my single-shot, I dropped the last duck in the now broken formation before the rest of the flock disappeared. I remember Dr. Boudry being quite impressed with my getting two birds from one flock, in flight, with two shots from a single-shot .410. That is likely one reason – and being a safe, careful hunter – that for years and years after, I was invited to hunt with Dr. Boudry and his family. I remember very well something that Dr. Boudry told me when we were sitting in a duck blind together on Partridge Lake. "Donny, the greatest thing the medical profession has going for itself is the recuperative powers of the human body."

Actually, my first wing shot was killing a Ruffed Grouse with my .22. I was hunting with my cousin Denis. He was carrying my .410 and I was carrying my .22. Our Cocker Spaniel, Dot, was tagging along and Dot flushed a Ruffed Grouse. The grouse flew directly behind an oak tree, which grouse have an uncanny knack of doing. I could not even see the bird when I pulled the trigger, but I flicked off a round and Denis yelled, "You got it!" The .22 pellet went under the left wing and out the neck. Pure luck. We also got a pheasant and a few squirrels that day. I often gutted my game on the spot because we often hunted all day in warm weather. That was probably something I learned from Butch or his father. Sometimes we even dry-plucked and singed our ducks while we were in the marsh watching for other ducks. To singe the ducks, we sometimes used our paper lunch bags or built a small fire of bulrushes or cattails. This way, the chore of cleaning ducks was already done when we got home after a full day of hunting. My youngest brother, Darren, who was younger than my son, is to this day nostalgic about the smells he associated with cleaning ducks in Papa's garage. I mixed paraffin with a little beeswax which floated in hot water. Adding the softer beeswax made the wax more pliable. Straight paraffin had a tendency to crumble. I used a Coleman camping stove to heat the wax-water dip. I dipped the mostly plucked duck in the wax water which coated the duck. Drawing the duck through the floating wax coated it in wax. In about a minute, the wax hardened. When the wax was peeled off, the pin feathers and the down feathers that were still attached to the bird came off with the sheets of wax. Voile – the bird looked like it just came out of the grocery store meat department.

Brother Dougie, five years older than Darren, floated some rivers with me, but he was also a little young for hunting with me, being born the year I graduated from high school.

During junior high school and high school, I also hunted with Jeff whose family rented our upstairs, with Ron who lived across the street, with Jerry who lived over by the ice house, with Bill who lived near Brainerd's bridge, with Glenn who lived west of town, but mostly, by far, with Butch. Classmates like Pete, Ted, and others, during deer season, stored their rifles or shotguns in their lockers during

school hours. Never had a problem, although we did not advertise our ploy, especially because my uncle was high school principal.

Whoever was my hunting partner, we got pretty good at double-teaming squirrels. If there was a squirrel sighted, we would run and tree it. We would stand together for a minute or so at the base of the tree, then one of us would walk directly away from the tree the squirrel was hiding in. Focused on the boy moving, the squirrel would move around the trunk or branch, disclosing its whereabouts to the probing eye of the stationary hunter looking up. If I was hunting alone, I would tree a squirrel, stand by the tree a minute or so, then throw my jacket out from the tree and the squirrel would usually move around from the side of the tree where the moving jacket came to rest. We always went for head shots – head shots or misses. That ploy meant no meat was wasted. Annette was my first date. It was a squirrel-hunting date. We were around fourteen or fifteen years old I think.

For squirrels, Bill and I scoured the Brainerd's Bridge area. Butch and I concentrated on the Shadow Lake Cemetery and South Park. Denis and I roamed the Bethany Home Care Center grounds. Glenn and I hunted the hills west of town. Protected areas seemed to have the best squirrel populations. But we were discreet – and we ran fast. One time Butch and I were hunting with Chuckie out at the Chain o' Lakes which are twenty-some lakes connected by canals and channels and ringed with cottages. The lakes vary in size from a few acres to some lakes that are a mile across. These spring-fed lakes are about four to six miles from Waupaca. It was just after Labor Day when the summer people families go back to their homes in Milwaukee, Chicago, Peoria, etc. Often, the wives and children of the family who owned the cottages would stay at their cottage all summer and the husbands would come up on the weekends. After Labor Day is when the local population drops from about 6,000 (May to Labor Day) back to 3,000 (Labor Day to May) residents. We were driving the winding roads past cottages looking for squirrels. Cottages, hundreds of them, now mostly empty until next Spring, ringed these beautiful lakes called "The Killarneys of America." The cottages averaged about thirty feet apart. Approximately one out of four cottages had feeders their owners or occupants kept filled all summer for their birds and our squirrels. Fat corn- and seed-fed delicious squirrels. The three of us were squirrel hunting in, and from, Chuck's Buick convertible. Top down of course. Chuck was driving, Butch was riding shotgun (figuratively and actually), and I was in the backseat. One, two, three or more hunters, whether by boat, skiff, or auto, only one gun was ever loaded at one time by our own self-imposed rule of safety. A squirrel was running across a wire that crossed over the road and Butch shot it. The squirrel dropped on the floor in the backseat next to me and Chuck never slowed the car down. One time, Butch shot a squirrel in a yard of a permanent resident. The owner started chasing Butch down the road. After a hundred yards or so, the guy yelled, "Is that you, Butch?" Butch yelled back over his shoulder, "Yah, is that you Mr. Thompson?" They stopped running, Butch got chewed out and after apologizing, we resumed our hunting.

Mom said several times that of all the game I brought home for our dinner table, she liked squirrels the best – as long as I cut them up. Squirrels were small enough to put in the frying pan whole, but Mom said they looked too much like little babies, so I was to cut them up.

Glenn and I hunted west of Waupaca, out where he lived on Highway 54. By the time I was about twelve or fourteen years old, Papa and I bought an 870 Remington "Wingmaster" 12 gauge from Ray, who was a local, rural tavern owner who also sold guns. It was exactly like Butch's! One of the first times Glenn and I were returning to his house after hunting the wooded hills around his house, it was dark and we were walking back to his house, down the road. I accidentally dropped my new shotgun on the road and broke the stock which was most devastating. Fortunately, Mr. Grant, a cabinet-maker, glued and clamped it. The butt plate was destroyed, so we put a Redhead rubber sleeve over the end of the stock. My dad never did find out, thank heavens. As far as I was concerned, Mr. Grant saved my life! I used that shotgun for about thirty years, until my son Mark took it to Alaska with him in 1980. He's lived in Sitka ever since 1980.

The Boudrys and I hunted and fished together for many years. We fished the spring "run" of white bass in the Wolf River from either Gill's or Guths's Landings, the walleye "runs," ice-fished trout in Lake Winnebago, Mirror Lake, and "the Chain." We had many great, most enjoyable outdoor fishing as well as hunting experiences.

Dr. Boudry had a boat-builder who lived across the street from our house on Jefferson Street build him a boat. It was a big, lapstrake rowboat that would take a big motor and several passengers with dogs and decoys. He called it the Mahebujo. The first two letters, Ma, were for his name, Marshall, his wife Mary, their daughter Mary; the next two letters, he, for their daughter Helen; the next two letters for Butch; and the last two letters for their son John. I am a very blessed man to have had the support of my Dad and Mom combined with the hunting and fishing tutoring and companionship of Dr. Boudry and his family. Invaluable memories. Wonderful people. Indelible inscriptions in my memory.

During my four years at Central State College immediately following high school which is thirty miles from Waupaca in Stevens Point, I did not do much hunting or fishing. I was studying, working on potato farms and convalescent centers, managing the Student Union, gardening for the college president, taking tickets and stocking shelves at the University Cafeteria, or driving school bus both early morning and late afternoon. I do remember "poking around" what is now called the Fred Schmeekle Nature Reserve for Ruffed Grouse. While I was in college, Mr. Schmeekle was my conservation major advisor. He was chairman of the Conservation Department and a very popular professor. Central State College had the first conservation major of any college or university in the United States. Later, I found out that my hero Aldo Leopold went to the first university that had a forestry degree, Yale. The Schmeekle Reserve is northwest of my old dorm in Stevens Point called Delzell Hall which was across from the hospital. I grouse hunted on the Schmeekle Reserve with my .410. The 12 gauge would be too loud in the City of Stevens Point. Most of the University of Wisconsin Stevens Point Campus is currently about a half-mile northwest of the "Old Main" building. "Old Main" was where classes, <u>all</u> classes at the college, were held when I attended school at Stevens Point (1955-1959). The new campus today is adjacent to the Fred Schmeekle Nature Reserve. Many of my friends at "Central State College" (CSC) which is what the university was called when I attended, were Korean War veterans. They were attending the university on the "G. I. Bill." These guys were at least four years older than I was, and decidedly more physically and, especially, more mentally mature.

SCS varsity sports teams – and most college and university teams for that matter during those days -- were comprised primarily of Korean War veterans. My Korean War veteran friend, Lew, took me for weekend duck hunts near his home in Nekoosa which is close to the Petenwell Flowage. Dave, my college roommate, hosted a few of us at his folks' cabin at Lake Nebagamon for a couple grouse hunt weekends in the cedar swamps, but over-all, I probably did more studying and working (and partying) than hunting during my college years at "Point." Come to think about it, many of my roommates were Korean War veterans.

During my junior year at Stevens Point, I had a very stimulating experience. Our ornithology class was going to go to Plainfield, WI and visit the Buena Vista Wildlife Refuge which was  being managed by Drs. Frederick and Frances Hamerstrom. Our assignment, after being instructed the evening before, was to sit in a three and one-half cubic foot bird blind – or bird hide -- and through little holes, extend our spotting scopes and/or binoculars and read the numbers and colors on the bands on the legs of the dancing Prairie Chickens. While or between the male Prairie Chickens dancing!

The late afternoon before the morning of our assignment, the Hamerstroms and their assistants showed our class members which blind or bird-hide to which we each were assigned. This orientation was important because we had to find our way in the dark the next morning and be in our blind before it got light in the east. There was a short six-inch stool to sit on. Our scopes were mostly twenty power on tripods. The male Prairie Chickens would arrive a little before sunup and begin their age-old dancing ritual to attract a female. Walt Disney calls it the "Sunrise Serenade." The males pounded their feet on the ground and made alluring, guttural sounds to attract the females. The entire "booming ground" was, say, forty yards in rough diameter. Each male had a square footage of approximately a couple hundred square feet within which he danced and boomed. The more aggressive males had larger, more centrally-located patches of ground that they defended with considerable flutterings and squawkings should an intruding male come close to the imaginary boundary line that only the defending male could see in his mind's eye. They also used their feet to tear at the intruder but seldom was permanent injury inflicted. Just a little blood and a few feathers usually.

It was a true "Sunrise Serenade" of the most animated sort! When the sun came up, the females would start arriving on the booming grounds. Then the tempo really picked up! Infrequently we would witness a copulation. By gathering the band numbers and colors of the bands on their legs, and sketching the approximate locations and sizes of the respective "stages" upon which the males performed, over the years the Hamerstrom's management of Buena Vista the Prairie Chickens grew in number. Burning to maintain a short grass prairie at the site of the traditional booming grounds was necessary. Keeping the booming grounds in short grass was critical. If the grass was more than a couple inches high, the birds would forsake their spring ritual or move to a close-cropped pasture elsewhere, if there was one.

I went back to the Hamerstroms a few times after graduating from college to help with their research. Dr. Fred and Dr. Fran Hamerstrom lived in a big, rustic house that was never painted. It was built just before the Civil War and the young men of the family, back then, went to war before they finished the house. The ball room on the second floor was not completed, the house was never painted – some say the young men never returned from the war – but it was a fitting backdrop to the Hamerstroms style and total dedication to their life's devotion. They had a ferret chained to a leg of their grand piano and Ambrose, their pet Great-Horned Owl, flew regular flight routes through the house. I marvel to think of the inspiration and experience afforded

many college students by the Hamerstroms over many years. When Frances was writing one of her books, **An Eagle to the Sky** she called and asked me if I would bring my son Mark to their place so she could get a photograph of a child climbing a tree for her book, which I did. Mark's picture is in her book. Another time, Harold, with whom I worked at the Milwaukee Public Museum was a security guard at the Museum an also an officer in the Wisconsin Society of Ornithology, and I went up to Plainfield for a spring weekend of camping at the Hamerstroms. When we were out exploring, we happened upon a Woodcock peenting and performing his spring courtship. We rushed back to the house and told Fran. She quickly threw the equipment into her Volkswagen bus and we hustled to the place we saw the "timberdoodle." We set up the mist nets, caught the Woodcock, weighed and banded him and released him. I recorded these events on 16mm movie film for the documentary movies I was producing for the Milwaukee Public Museum. When I asked Fran how she would like me to describe her vehicle during my lectures when I showed her VW bus, she said, "Just tell your audiences that I have a typical woman's vehicle. You know, rats and mice for bait, traps for kestrels and other critters, aluminum poles for mist nets, scales for weighing, tapes for measuring – just the regular things."

Being too young to enlist for Korea and too old for Viet Nam, to do my part for my country militarily I joined the U. S. Army National Guards while attending college. That meant attending weekly meetings and the two-week summer camps in Stevens Point or Waupaca, later in Detroit. My father was my Commanding Officer in Wisconsin – he was CO for Waupaca,

Wisconsin Rapids, and Appleton – and I joined at Stevens Point and attended several substitute weekly meetings and summer camps with the Waupaca National Guards. I was in the Fire Direction Center for 4.2 inch mortars in Waupaca and Forward Observer for the 155mm howitzers in Stevens Point. I especially liked the Firing Range. Today I am very hard of hearing, I think as a result of those experiences and explosions and all my hunting, trap shooting, target shooting, fireworks, listening to loud music, and having loud cars with no ear protection!

I regret not wearing ear protection. Young people will regret standing in front of the speakers at concerts when they get older.

During my attending the universities of Wisconsin and Michigan, Dr. and Mrs. Boudry's sons and daughters also graduated from universities, got married and later brought their spouses back to Waupaca to hunt and fish. Our hunting party about quintupled. We all hunted ducks and deer together. Deer we hunted primarily at the "Boar's Nest." John, Butch's older brother, and his wife Shirley bought a deserted farm and planted most of it to pine trees. Located west of Waupaca, it was barely into Portage County where rifles were legal for hunting deer. Elsewhere, in more populated counties in central Wisconsin, like Waupaca County, only shotguns with slugs were legal. What memories we have of the "Boar's Nest!"

The garage at "the Nest" was a veritable butcher's shop. It was complete with meat hooks, stainless steel tables, meat saws and knives, rolls of butcher paper, tape and marking pens, meat grinders, freezers – in short, anything and everything you needed to process deer. Sometimes the deer were wrapped and in the freezer before the body heat was out of them.

While attending college at Stevens Point I occasionally drove the thirty miles home to Waupaca to do my laundry and get some good home-cooking probably once a month, sometimes more often if I missed the weekly National Guard meetings in Stevens Point on Monday nights. If I missed a Guard meeting in Stevens Point one week, I would drive to Waupaca to make up for it, maybe going to meetings twice the next week, one in Waupaca and one in Stevens Point.

On one of these "substitute" Guard trips home, David and Dale told me of an experience they had down at Boudry's duck pond. It was April and there was still ice in the middle of Mirror Lake. Walking along the edge of Boudry's pond, Dale spotted a big Northern Pike spawning in the shallow water of the pond. He said, "David! Jump on it!" David said, "No, Dale, you saw it first, you jump on it." Dale said, "No, you. You're bigger!" Neither boy, David aged sixteen or Dale fourteen, was eager to jump into the cold water. Still, how often do you get a chance to "get" a huge Northern Pike? By this time, Mrs. Boudry is up the hill at their dining room bay windows, looking down at the boys about a hundred yards down the hill who were on the edge of their pond. David jumps the fish with a full body press and face plant, combined with an arm-leg squeeze! Mrs. Boudry yells, "Marshall, come quick, one of the Danielson boys is drowning in our pond!" Dr. Boudry calmly came to the window -- he was calm in everything he did -- and about this time a fifty inch Northern Pike comes flailing through the air and lands in the grass. Dr. Boudry said, "No, Mary, that's just the Danielson boys doing some spring fishing." David and Dale took the fish up to our house. David put on dry clothes, then asked Pop if they could borrow the mail route car for a while, to which Papa acquiesced. The boys knew there was an early fishing contest open on the Wolf River. On the way to Gill's Landing, they realized there was no evidence of the fish being caught – hooked in the jaw for example. When they got to where the contest was, they rooted around Pop's car  and found an old identification bracelet that had sister Debbie's name on it under the seat, so they wore a hole in the fish's jaw to simulate where a hook could've been. They entered the fish in the contest and won!

Their questionable fishing escapade reminded me of our Grampa Eddy. He worked in Sheboygan at a plastics company. G'pa liked to fish for muskies. He cut a quarter-inch thick piece of transparent Lucite plastic into a slab that measured about four-by-six inches. Then he would drown out a gopher – pour water down a gopher hole until the soggy gopher had to come out or drown. Gramps would put the gopher in a pail and go fishing. He hooked the gopher in a hind leg, put the gopher on the plastic slab and tied the floating devise to the back of his boat. The hook was connected to his fish rod by the fishing line. He would row his boat along shoreline early or late in the day before or after work. When he saw a swirl in the water behind the gopher who did not want to get wet again, G'pa would reach over, yank the cord that was attached to the plastic "raft." The gopher would start swimming. Often as not, the musky would strike! Sometimes a Northern Pike.

From 1959 to 1963, following college and receiving a four-year Bachelor of Science degree, my young family lived in a factory suburb of Detroit, Michigan where I taught school. Detroit needed science teachers and paid a $1000 "signing bonus" to first year science teachers who signed a one-year contract to teach for them. My first annual contract was for $4650 and my classmates who went into teaching that same year averaged $3500. Almost every day during pheasant season for a couple years, five of us junior high school teachers – Don taught Industrial Arts, Jim and Harry taught math, John taught social studies and I taught science – would be dressed and ready for the field when the bell rung at 3:15PM. Classes were dismissed at 2:50PM and the building was to be vacated by 3:15PM, unless there were special circumstances like meetings. Since we left the building with our hunting togs on at 3:15PM, about twenty minutes later we would drive to Berville and be hunting. The five of us would meet Harry whose Dad had close connections in the Berville, MN township north of Detroit. We always got a couple pheasants and sometimes more. Believe it or not, we mostly hunted the cauliflower fields and drainage ditches. One of my most prized possessions is an arm patch Jim had made for us that says, "Berville Hunting Association." We "Five Amigos" camped, hunted and cavorted together. Jim was also our barber. $2 per haircut. In college one day, he cut twenty heads of hair for $1 per head. That was good money in the fifties when we were in college!

Pte. Mouillee Waterfowl Reserve is on the western end of Lake Erie and was a favorite haunt of ours for duck hunting. Also, it was between Toledo and Detroit. Besides hunting, there were duck-calling contests, decoy-layout shooting contests, pumpkin-seed and skirted "big water" skiff shoot offs, duck identification contests, punt gun demonstrations, and usually during duck hunting season a good population of wildfowl spread over many square miles of bays, islands, and wild rice to hunt. The punt gun demonstrations were most interesting. Years ago when hunters thought the game and land and trees were inexhaustible, market hunters would <u>swim</u> their punt boats, keeping a low profile on the blind side of the boat, out to a raft of ducks. Usually diving ducks. The punt gun was a large bore, huge gauge, more like a two-inch pipe. When the hunter got within range and the ducks were starting to get spooky, he would reach up and pull the trigger. The butt of the gun was positioned against a padded and weighted seat, the barrel hung out over the bow. The "shot" that was propelled by a large charge of powder was nails, bolts, pieces of chain – most anything of

metal that would act like shrapnel. The "shot" would cut a huge swath into the raft of ducks. The boat would be propelled backwards several feet by the blast. Usually,

an accomplice in a smaller skiff, would pick up the swimmer/shooter and the two of them would retrieve the dead ducks after finishing-off the wounded ones. Over one hundred ducks were commonly gathered with each punt gun blast! Of course, in the demonstration, no ducks were killed. But there was a lot of churned-up water!

Our fivesome did not hunt deer in Michigan at that time. I'm not sure why we didn't.

But we certainly pursued the pheasants and waterfowl! Squirrels and woodcock also.

What we shot wound up on our tables. "If we shot it, we ate it," was our creed!

Not familiar with mergansers (fish ducks), I shot one while we were hunting Pte. Mouillee. When my wife roasted the merganser, the gamey smell of fish almost drove us out of the house. But I shot it, therefore we were going to eat it. She and I could barely get a few bites of the breast down, but our two-year old son Mark picked at the carcass while sitting in his high chair until he had cleaned-off most of the carcass!

While teaching science my first year to seventh, eighth, and ninth grade students in Detroit, I was awarded a National Science Foundation Award for "Innovative Science Teaching" ($1000 and several graduate courses at the school(s) of my choice). I parlayed the award into a Master's Degree at the University of Michigan. The first and basic classes were held at night in downtown Detroit's Wayne State University, an affiliate of the University of Michigan. Then I went to summer school in Ann Arbor, the main University of Michigan campus. It was here that

I was introduced to Aldo Leopold who remains one of my three favorite authors over these past sixty adult years. Near the end of fulfilling my Master of Science degree requirements, I was asked to assist three professors who were teaching at the U of MI. I was also taking classes during these summers in the School of Natural Resources. Assisting professors, especially as famous as these three were, was good for my resume'. One professor I assisted taught Environmental Education, Richard L. Weaver, and was an Aldo Leopold scholar (which I also became). I completed my Master's Degree thesis under Dr. Weaver – "An Analysis of the State-Produced Conservation Education Materials." Another professor taught Fishery Resources. He is the internationally famous Karl Lagler who authored Fishes of the Great Lakes. I conducted bag-seining studies of fishes along the shores of Lake Erie for Dr. Lagler. On one trip but unknown to me at the time, a graduate student wrapped a huge carp in the wet bag seine and when we got back to the campus, he released the carp in the fancy pedestal pool. The summer school students fed the fish all summer. The third professor I assisted, Dr. Stan Cain, became Under Secretary of the Department of the Interior. I helped Dr. Cain with fieldtrips taking students to the Muskingham Watershed in Ohio. I had a chance to drive the largest steam shovel in the world that was used at the open pit mines. Two pick-up trucks, side-by-side, would fit in the bucket of the steam shovel. By this time in my life, I reminisced about my family on Mirror Lake and hunting with Butch and his family. Returning to Wisconsin, now that my family was underway with a son and a daughter and after four years in Michigan, started looking more attractive every week.

An opportunity to return to Wisconsin came in the form of a job opening in 1963 at the newly constructed, multi-million-dollar Milwaukee Public Museum (MPM). It is the fourth largest Natural History Museum in the United States – now, one of the most up-to-date with graphics, color, interactive and interpretive displays. Carl Akeley who worked at the MPM during its formative years is credited with building the first ecologically complete diorama ever to appear in a museum anywhere in the world. He worked in the Taxidermy Department and his diorama featured the muskrat in its natural environment. Mr. Akeley showed a perky muskrat near the entrance to its muskrat house, in the water of course, at the edge of a marsh. Prior to this breakthrough exhibit and technique, birds and other animals were shown on a perch or piece of driftwood. Mr. Akeley showed the entire natural history of the muskrat in his complete diorama of this furbearing marsh animal.

After a couple interviews, tests and screenings, I emerged as the Museum Search Committee's first choice. Our family of four -- the papa, the mama, the three-year old son, the one-year old daughter -- loaded up a small U-Haul trailer with our worldly possessions in Detroit. We pulled the trailer 400 miles to Milwaukee with our 1958 Pontiac station wagon and arrived in Milwaukee well after midnight. The morning sun awakened us. We had slept much of the night in the car in Lincoln Park on the south side of Milwaukee after an all-night drive. When we awoke, Mark said, "Let's go home now." Kay said, "Honey, we don't have a home anymore."

However, that day we found an upstairs two-bedroom apartment north of downtown Milwaukee near Silver Spring

Drive and Green Bay Avenue on Long Island Drive. We were helped in our unloading by cousin Bob and his wife Rita. Bob taught in Greendale, south and west of downtown Milwaukee and he became one of our hunting group. It was so good to be back in Wisconsin!

It was August. Dr. Boudry heard about this guy who had a fiber glass company in Ixonia, near Manawa (Waupaca County), and was building fourteen-foot skiffs that weighed  about forty pounds for $125. Butch and I both bought one.

Daughter Maria came along after we were in Milwaukee about six months. Because our family of five now rented an upstairs apartment in Milwaukee, the only place to store our skiff was in the stairwell. Luckily, the fire marshal never came to visit. The skiff had a "cockpit" that two small adults like Butch and me could fit it, like when we floated the rivers. Or like when one of my brothers, often David or Dale, sometimes Dougie, would float with me during duck season. Normally, we reminded each other not to lean sideways when we came upon a barbed wire crossing the river. Although it was illegal, many farmers would string a wire across the navigable rivers to control their cattle. Twice, once with Dale, once with David, we capsized because we did not follow our own advice and leaned to the side or grabbed the wire instead of leaning forward or aft. Both Dale and David dived for our shotguns and shells. We eventually caught up with the floating ducks we had in the skiff when we went over. This capsizing happened twice. The same spot. Behind Gunderson's on the Crystal River downstream from the Waupaca Conservation Club in the town of Little Hope near the Red Mill.

Butch and I both used our own skiffs when we hunted lakes and marshes together so we could spread out and cover a larger area. Also, we could carry our decoys and dogs. We both outfitted our skiffs which were intended to be paddled or poled, with oarlocks. It was much more efficient to row across open water than paddle across it – and it was also less fatiguing. Joe was a master carpenter at the Milwaukee Public Museum and offered to build my oarlocks, so I took my skiff to work one day. What an ingenious job he did. I could pull on my oars so hard that I could lift the skiff up on thin ice and break through. I needed to do this a few times when I would hunt longer than I should have and ice would form.

After about a year renting in Milwaukee, we found a house in Bayview on the south side of Milwaukee, across from South Shore Park, on the shore of Lake Michigan. It was an old Victorian house with much character. We had our family, our house, and we were back in Wisconsin closer to our folks who lived in Waupaca – my folks -- and LaCrosse – her folks. Back with family and longtime friends. Life is good! Hunting and fishing is good also!

My first kill with an arrow in Wisconsin was my first year back in Wisconsin. Leon was the Radio-TV Producer for the Milwaukee Public Museum (MPM) and he lived north and west of downtown Milwaukee about twenty miles or thereabouts in a village called Granville. After work one evening we went bow hunting. On the way back to his house, a small deer jumped up, ran quartering away and at about twenty yards I got a heart shot. It seems that I led the deer about twelve feet. Leon was duly impressed. I was very lucky.

Butch and I were again hunting and fishing together! A four-year hiatus, but a dream come true! Our regular haunts resumed, we were floating the rivers around Waupaca, like the Crystal and Waupaca Rivers; hunting and ice-fishing Lake Winnebago. Butch and Joan were now living in Neenah, two blocks from Lake Winnebago. We again were hunting Lake Poygan, the Chain o' Lakes, other local ponds, lakes, and rivers and especially Partridge Lake just outside of Fremont. Dr. Boudry owned some of this very shallow lakeshore in its northwest corner. I know firsthand it is shallow, having "booted over" in it. Leaning way over on the side rail of my light-weight skiff one Saturday morning, I touched off a round at a Baldpate, got the duck, but rolled the skiff over and ended up standing in about three feet of water and "loon." I thought it would be over my head. Nearby hunters came to my rescue. They emptied my skiff of water and helped me crawl back into my skiff, after I dived for my gun, and shells (the few I could locate in the "loon"), but at least my lunch floated!

One day, probably when duck hunting was about to close for the season in 1963, my first year back in Wisconsin, Butch said, "Donny, you've hunted deer with a bow, why don't you get a rifle and deer hunt with our family this year?" No more welcomed words of invitation had ever assailed my ears! So, I started making inquiries about a rifle. I asked the best big game hunters in the world for their recommendations. I knew them! I worked with them daily!

Working at the Milwaukee Public Museum with co-workers who had been all over the world collecting big game as well as small game for the Museum's displays and dioramas, I knew the best hunters there were! I asked them what caliber rifle they would recommend for Wisconsin deer hunting? Their consensus was a 30.06 because it was so versatile. Many sizes of bullets and charges of powder for different muzzle velocities, trajectories, and impacts. Then I started looking for a 30.06. Lady Luck was with me. My best friend at the museum, Bill, worked in the Taxidermy Department. He told me that Walter, the Chief of Taxidermy who had also been all over the world hunting big game for the Museum told him to tell Don that he had a 30.06 he might part with.

Bill and I spent most every noon hour carving decoys while eating our lunches. He was THE master carver. I learned more from Bill about hunting and carving than I ever could from any other ten men.

At coffee break the next day I asked Walter if he indeed would sell me his rifle, for how much would he sell it if he would sell it, and what were the specifications of the rifle in question. It was a 30.06. Optics, variable Bushnell Scope. Make, Husqvarna (Swedish, Mauser-action, bolt action, five-shot clip). Even had a hand-engraved leather sling. $100! Are you kidding me? About the best deal ever offered, one hunter to another, in the history of mankind's hunting! Back then, 1963, it was easily worth $500. This rifle had bagged big game in Alaska, Africa, India, the "Lower

48," and elsewhere. I bought it! I was happy to the utmost! Now to get my first deer with a rifle. With Butch's family no less!

On a Friday afternoon after work – with opening day for deer the following morning – I left Milwaukee and drove north 120 miles to Waupaca. Butch was already at the Boar's Nest when I arrived. Butch's older brother and his wife Jake bought the farm the family now called the "Boar's Nest" a couple years previously. Previously mentioned, they planted much of the farm to pine tree seedlings. They also owned the Stedman farm over on Highway 54, also planted to pines. Portage, Waupaca, and Jackson Counties were historically the three counties that vied for most deer taken each year in Wisconsin.

While walking the "Boar's Nest" property with Butch that Friday evening before opening day for deer which loomed in about twelve hours, Butch pointed out where he and the rest of the family members would be located. They all had their hunting spots picked out on the east end of the farm having hunted the farm for a few years already. Dr. Boudry had a pit blind that he dug so only his head and shoulders were above ground. I could pick my spot from sites that were left. I chose a spot in the woods, over on the west end of the farm. I was the only hunter of our party hunting the west half of the "Boar's Nest" property. I chose a spot just below the crest of a rise, in the woods, so I would not be silhouetted against the sky. The breeze, according to tomorrow's weather report, would be blowing from the scrapes and trails toward me as the deer would come from the corn fields to the west, at least in the morning.

After reconnoitering the farm with Butch, I now felt oriented well enough to find my way back to my spot the next morning in the dark. It was approximately a half mile walk from the "Boar's Nest" house and garage to my deer stand.

About an hour after settling in and about one minute after the legal opening minute, four does came down the trail at me. I said to myself, not yet Don, and let them pass through. There were going to be several does shot this weekend by our group. The biggest doe came back about fifteen minutes later and I dropped her, dressed her out, she was dry, and I put a branch over her so she was not conspicuous. Then I settled down once more. Other deer passed through, but no bucks. Around eleven o'clock along comes a nice, inquisitive buck. Nose to the ground. Stops. Sniffs under the branch I laid across the doe. I made a squeak-sound with pursed lips. He snaps his head up and looks straight at me. Quick, easy shot. Eight points eastern. My first buck with a rifle and it's not even noon yet on Opening Day!

With two shots already from my direction, the only hunter in the western half of John's posted property, I figured I was in for some teasing for missing a couple shots. After dressing out the buck and hanging him in the pines alongside the doe, I went in for lunch about one o'clock. We agreed to come for lunch about one o'clock because many hunters go for lunch at noon or earlier. They moved deer around when going in for lunch, so we took advantage of their activity. I went for lunch empty-handed because rather than drag the two deer in, I figured to come back after lunch with Dr. Boudry's Bronco to get the deer.

Mrs. Boudry usually made ox-tail soup for "Opening Day Lunch." After getting good-naturedly teased about not being able to hit anything -- my fellow hunters around the table did not know I had two deer dressed and hanging in the pines -- Lou got up from the table to get something to drink. We had an unwritten rule that no alcohol consumption during hunting hours. Beware after sundown. Lou is the friend who was giving me the most grief about not getting anything with two shots. (He should have checked under my finger nails.) So, I slipped part of the male deer's anatomy into Lou's bowl of soup when he left the table to get a pop. Most of us knew what part of the deer I slipped into Lou's soup. We were watching Lou out of the corners of our eyes. He was struggling with what he called the "gristle-like 'pointy-end' of the ox tail." He apparently did not know that ox-tail soup was made from cross-sections of the tail, no "pointy-ends." When he realized, finally, thanks to Mrs. Boudry, what it was that was in his soup, we all burst out laughing. Lou now knew and he took off after me!

When my brother Dale got married, he arranged for a wedding dinner the evening before the wedding for our family and friends at Simpson's Restaurant in Waupaca. My daughter Maria was about four years old, it was in the mid-sixties and Maria was sitting about six chairs down from me. Maria waved at me, trying to catch my eye. I asked Maria what she wanted. She said, "What kind of meat is this, Papa?" I told her it was chicken. She said, "What is chicken?" When I told her it was like pheasant, she said, "Oh, good! I like pheasant." Our son and daughters were more accustomed to grouse and venison than chicken and beef.

Seventeen years went by. I had not seen Lou since the "soup episode." I lived in Milwaukee and was divorced and remarried.

Walking down Main Street with my new wife who I met in Alaska, I was showing Lady Phyllis the downtown Waupaca where I grew up. "Here's where I bought hunting supplies," "Here's where I got caught shop-lifting," "This was our favorite restaurant," "I went to the barber down there, under the Pool Hall." Guess who is coming down the street toward us? Lou! He's about a block away. When we got close enough, I said, "Hi, Lou! This is Lady Phyllis, my new wife." He obviously hadn't forgotten our Ox Tail Soup lunch experience even after seventeen years! He just looked at me, smiled, shook his head and the only thing he said was, "You s.o.b!" He did not use abbreviations. Then he resumed walking. Phyllis was scratching her head.

(Snippet. On January 12, 2019 I was coursing through my iPhone messages. This is more than fifty years since the person with the same surname as Lou – a distinctive last name – had responded to another person's email who was from Waupaca. I asked this person in a response message if he was related to Lou. I left my phone number in my message and a few minutes later he called. He was Lou's son and had also hunted with his father at the "Boar's Nest." What floored me was this son, Bryon, not only hunted with the Boudrys, but knew the story of the "Oxtail Soup." Lou passed away about fifteen years ago, but also passed along the "Oxtail Soup Story" to his son.)

Phyllis and I met counting Bald Eagles in the Chilkat River Valley of Alaska, near Haines. It was an Audubon-sponsored fieldtrip and truly a once in a lifetime experience. Between 3000 and 4000 Bald Eagles on a four mile stretch of the Chilkat River near Haines, AK. Since time immemorial, Bald Eagles have funneled from western Siberia and Greenland to the east, according to bird banding records, into the Chilkat River bottoms for their winter. Mild weather, sanctuary, plenty of food. Most of the eagles arrive in late October and after spending the winter feeding on chum salmon, then leave the Chilkat environs around the months of March and April for their mating and nesting rituals.

The Chilkat River has its beginnings in the icefields and glaciers. During the spring melt, the river, especially at its headwaters, is deep and turbulent. This is when the salmon fight their way upstream to their ancient spawning grounds. Brown bears intercept a few of the salmon. After the older salmon spawn, their natural history claims their lives and they expire while floating downstream. As the salmon get closer and closer to the ocean, the river channel spreads out. Actually, the river per se becomes hundreds of shallow channels and rivulets that meander through sand flats more than a mile wide near the ocean. Since the river is now slow and shallow, especially starting in, say, August, the dead and dying fish become mired or stuck in the sand. For the next half year or so, the rivulets re-weave and re-braid their channels, exposing fresh, frozen fish all winter long for the eagles to eat. It was in this setting that about twenty of us who worked for or associated with the National Audubon Society were invited to document and photograph the Bald Eagles.

My first wife and I were separated after twenty years. My new wife, Phyllis, was a member of our "Eagle Entourage." She was divorced and had six children. Phyllis was a knock-down, jaw-dropping, knee-knocking, beautiful redhead. Blue ribbon type. Her more outstanding characteristics were her kindness, honesty, and innocence; besides being a brilliant person. Although neither she nor I were seeking companionship, I was smitten. And, she had answers to questions I had sought answers to all my life! Phyllis had been a member of the Church of Jesus Christ of Latter-Day Saints for about twenty years. She was born into a Methodist family in the hills of West Virginia, grew up in New Jersey and attended Brigham Young University in Provo, Utah. She was of British stock, philosophically a non-hunter, but encouraged me in all of my interests and is the only one who ever made grouse gravy that I know of. More than once! But she will not eat wild game for reasons that I honor and she honors my desire to hunt.

In later deer hunting years at the "Boar's Nest," I hunted from another spot, a big horizontal limb about fifteen feet up in a huge red oak tree. It was in the corner where John's property joined property owned by a Mr. Migas. John told me Mr. Migas owned the IGA grocery store in Amherst Junction, so during the off-season I wrote Mr. Migas a letter asking him if I could sit in his tree for deer hunting. He responded with a very cordial letter giving me permission to hunt all of his property anytime any year. The first year I hunted out of the oak in what became known as "the Migas tree," I had crawled up into the tree in the early morning before dark. About the time the season opened, I saw John going to his stand and he saw me. John was at the other end of the pine plantation field of seedlings, about 200-300 yards away. An eight-point buck stepped out from right under my tree! I neither heard nor saw the deer. John stopped walking and pointed. I looked down, straight down. Slowly, I lowered my "Pelzer rifle," eased off the safety and pulled the trigger. The deer dropped like he was pole-axed and never even quivered. John gave a thumbs-up. In a typical first morning of deer hunting, I would count the number of shots during the first fifteen minutes each season. The number was always between fifty and ninety. The first fifteen minutes! That same morning there was a rifle shot behind me. A doe came limping along and disappeared into the pines that were about fifteen feet tall behind me. There was one opening in the pines that I could see. If the wounded doe passed through that opening, I could dispatch her. Otherwise she might suffer until dead. As it unfurled, she did in fact start to pass through this small opening. All I could see was her head so I shot. When the hunter who was tracking her came to the fence line about ten minutes later, he knew John's land was posted, but was also trying to be just and humane. When he asked me if he could track the doe he injured, I told him where the deer was laying – in so many rows of pine trees. The hunter thanked me and I thanked him for being a conscientious hunter.

Our three children pretty much grew up eating wild game, especially in their younger years. Matter-of-fact, when my friend and fellow grouse hunter George who was Field Editor of the National and International Wildlife Federation Magazines wanted some wild game for a special get together he called me. "Don, do you have any wild

game that I could have so I can make some 'wild game hors d'oeuvres' for our wildlife meeting we are having in Washington, D. C. next week?" He drove out to our place on the Blue Goose Road and I gave him some duck, goose, deer, bear (from a friend), antelope, and squirrel. He said his bosses were duly impressed with his canapes and that several of the attendees told George they tasted a few of the finger sandwiches with wild meat they had never tried before. On one of our "Wood Tick Weekends," George wrote an "Outdoor Emergency" article for the National Wildlife Magazine and a couple of us ended up being the centerfold of the November 1975 issue!

Through my good friend, Bud, I met another friend named Hans. Hans was a very big, muscular Kraut who had a thick German accent. Hans was a boat-builder and also lived in a big house near the South Shore Yacht Club with his wife Ruth. He was an old-world, master craftsman boat builder, specializing in yachts of the finest order. Hans and Ruth became very good friends of our family. Mutual friends, our trap shooting teams, fellow hunters, we had some marvelous sailing experiences on Hans' and Dr. Blackwood's yachts. For example, we participated in the "Queen's Cup" race for sail boats. The course was Milwaukee to Chicago to Muskegon, MI and back to Milwaukee. One time when we were running with the wind and the spinnaker was in full fill, we broached. Fortunately, the boat rights itself after capsizing. Nevertheless, it is scary to see a forty foot mast laying horizontal on the top of a foamy sea when you are hanging on for dear life and the boat is on its side!

Across Wentworth Avenue where we lived in Bayview, south

of downtown Milwaukee, an avid sportsman named Ken lived. He talked me into driving up to Mercer, WI where a guy named Bill Tutt owned the Flam-Bow Resort on the Flambeau Flowage. Tutt was a bear (with bow) and fishing guide. Tutt's wife was Fred Bear's daughter. Bud and Tutt and Marge and I became very good friends. Bill gave me a booklet of poems on the Northwoods that he wrote. He was a very proficient poet in my opinion. I will forever be indebted to Ken B. for introducing me to Tutt because then I introduced Bud to Tutt and we had some marvelous times together. Elaboration forthcoming.

I had just returned from an Audubon meeting a couple months previously in St. Louis where another friend who also worked for Audubon, Jay is his name, asked if I wanted to come to his home state of Wyoming where he was stationed. He was Vice President of the National Audubon Society for Audubon's Western Region. **Come Autumn,** Jay said, we could have a good antelope and elk hunt. I told him I couldn't afford an elk license, but he fixed me up with a resident antelope tag which was $5. I asked Hans if he wanted to go with me. He jumped at the chance and we took his plush motor home. Hans got a non-resident antelope and elk license. We hunted elk near the Tetons with Jay. Our first day of hunting, Hans and Jay told me to shoot an elk if I saw one, but I did not, nor did they. About sundown, we looked across this valley that we had to cross to get back to Jay's car. Four men and four horses were being unloaded from a four-horse trailer pulled by a very official-looking pick-up, forest green truck, with government decals on the doors. Jay said, "Be sure your rifles are unloaded," which they were. The four wardens came thundering up, skidded their horses to a stop, and proceeded to intimidate us -- or at least try to intimidate us. Hans is a big, six-foot four inch, two hundred and fifty-pound German who does not intimidate. We were being accused of hunting on federal land. Jay told them our guns were unloaded and we were merely crossing federal land (the Tetons) to get to private land. Hans chimed in also. The spokesman warden got in Hans' face. Hans had his rifle cradled in his right arm. The louder the warden yelled at Hans, the further back Hans leaned, elevating his rifle. His rifle was now between the warden's legs and Hans almost lifted him off the ground. The warden's voice squeaked, Jay made his case, Jay was right, the wardens saddled up and left. Regulations allowed hunters to cross federal land to get to their hunting land with unloaded rifles. Jay read them the regulations.

The next day we were going to get an antelope or two, or at least try. Hans got the first one. Jay and I were the "birddogs" that pushed a herd of antelopes past Hans and he picked out a nice male. These antelope were too spooked to get close to them for another shot, so Jay said, "Not much daylight left, so let's go over to my friend's place because he has antelope on his ranch." His friend also had a two-seater bi-plane with Browning shotguns strapped to the wing struts. The two guns converged in front of the plane at about seventy yards. He hunted coyotes with his airplane. His triggering device, to fire the two shotguns simultaneously, one on each side of the plane at the same time was ingenious. He used a garage door opener he called a solenoid.

Jay's farmer friend told me to go out behind the barn about 300 yards and "hunker down" in the brush while the three of them went in the house and drank coffee. He said that often he saw a herd of antelope go into an arroyo frequently about this time of day to bed down for the night. There was about twenty minutes of hunting left in the day – the sun was on the western horizon. Sure enough, a good-sized herd of antelope came up behind me, did not see me, and swung down into the canyon about 300 yards away. I tried sneaking, but quickly got my knees and hands full of cactus needles. All the antelope except one was down in the arroyo – and that one was watching me. On the other side of the arroyo and on the other side of the herd of antelope about forty yards from the antelope herd, if I guessed their location correctly, was a flat rock about ten feet in diameter. I hit the rock dead center with a 30.06 180 grain projectile and those antelope virtually squirted out of that water-carved canyon and came right at me!

I picked what looked like the biggest one of about twenty animals, so now both Hans and I had our antelopes.

That night we parked the motorhome at a wayside in an exceedingly remote section of very rural Wyoming. Hans was taking a shower and I was making supper. There was a knock at the door. Out where there was nothing – no houses, highways, nothing. It was a sheriff. He wanted to know if the motor home was mine. I said it belonged to my friend who was in the shower. The sheriff said, "Get your friend out here right now!" I said, "In a minute. He's probably drying off since the shower just quit." The sheriff said, "Well, he's lucky, because I mean 'right now'." So, Hans steps out and says, "Hello, what do you want?" The warden says, "I'm the sheriff and I'm here to arrest you." I can sense the hackles rising on the back of Hans' neck! The sheriff follows with,

"There is fresh blood dripping from the two deer hanging on the back of your motor home." (They were antelopes.) In his thickest German vernacular, Hans said, "Yah, ven you shoot and field dress animals, dey bleed." The sheriff did not think the season was open for antelope, even after Hans showed him the regulations. The sheriff went out to his fully-equipped squad car and called for backup. A little while later, we see red lights flashing and two more squad cars pulled into the wayside.

Sensing that something interesting was going to happen – maybe something exciting, I eased out the driver's side door with my camera and went around the motorhome – it was very dark and I got behind the officers who did not see me. They were standing at the side door of the motorhome, silhouetted in the light from the motorhome. There was a big rock across from the side-door, fortunately, that I stood behind. One or two of the officers had their hands on their sidearms as I recall and one of them knocked on the door, probably the first official to pay us a visit. Hans opened the door. He looked like a prize-fighter dressed in skivvies and a towel draped around his neck. In retrospect, I question the wisdom of what I did next, but I couldn't help myself. Here's gigantic Hans, backlighted and towering over the guys in front of him, at least one of whom has his handgun readied.

I touched-off my camera. It was a flash camera. It was very dark and the flash was so blinding, the three officers dived for cover! To avoid being shot at, I yelled "It was just a flash camera!" The season for antelope was indeed open, they did apologize, and all ended well. The photograph is easily one of my all-time favorites!

Driving north after work on Friday from the Milwaukee Public

Museum became a routine most every Friday after work from September until about Chistmas. Owning our house in Bayview, south of downtown, meant the possibility of having a hunting dog.

Someone at the Museum said that a world-famous retriever trainer lived about fifty miles west of Milwaukee. I drove out to Eagle, WI to meet Orin, renowned retriever dog trainer. Orin and I had immediate chemistry but there wasn't any way (1964) I could afford $1000 for one of his dogs. I wanted a Black Labrador female very badly. Orin said in his  opinion, the females are the best hunters. Females are less interested in sniffing "fingerprints" than hunting. "Females follow the scent of birds. Males follow the scent of females." Orin also bred, raised and trained Golden Retrievers and "knotheads" (that's what he called Chesapeake Bay Retrievers). He also had a few Water Spaniels. Orin had up to 100 dogs in his kennels at any one time that he was training, dogs from all over the world. "Red" was his only helper besides his wife and children. Orin's licensed game farm also included hawks, owls, 'coons, possums, foxes, wolves and other wildlife to care for – which later became very important in my Museum movie producing documentaries, Museum workshops for youth and our television show "Outdoor Reports."

Orin was very busy and needed more help. At least that is what I hoped.

Therefore, I asked Orin if I could "work off" some of the cost of a pup by helping him train dogs. He agreed. After working a short time for Orin, I selected a puppy who was a "no nonsense little girl" when separated from her litter mates. She was the first (and only pup of the litter) to pick up a scent after I dragged a piece of liver across the grass before Orin let the pups out of the kennel. She was eight weeks old. Good girl! Magna cum Laude! "Maggie!" Orin and I became good friends while training dogs and I learned lots. One of Orin's maxims about training dogs was, "Don't start too early. Dogs will be puppies only once in their lives." Orin also introduced me to James Lamb Free's book, <u>Training Your Retriever</u>. As I recall, the beginning of the book starts with Mr. Free stating that his book is written by an impatient man for impatient men who want immediate results with their training. That captured my attention. That was me. To this day, I believe it is the best DIY book on retriever training, but there are more recent books on the topic. Dave Duffy also has a good book out. Probably others by now.

One of Orin's prize-winning students was a young, eager Chesapeake Bay Retriever. The only problem with the dog was its eagerness. It didn't have time to sit squarely on the ground and wait for the signal to "mark" or "fetch." Orin and the judges wanted the dog's butt on the ground, firmly on the ground. Otherwise, points off. Orin did not want to spoil the dog's drive or spirits, nor did he want to have the dog penalized for its exuberance. Therefore, when he was training the dog to "screw his behind into the earth," Orin said "sit." If the dog did not emphatically sit, Orin would clamp the dog's ear in his Zippo cigarette lighter until the dog squealed. A couple "Zippo Lessons" was all it took. Now, the pudding's proof would be when he and the dog were actually in a Field Trial being judged. Orin had his right hand in his right pocket. When he said "Sit!" and the dog did not have his all into obeying, Orin would open the Zippo that was inside his pocket – right next to the dog's left ear! The dog responded to the ever so slight click.

Much of Orin's reputation as a retriever trainer came from his unparalleled success in Retriever Dog Trials. He won many "Best of Show" and "Blue Ribbons" with dogs from his kennel – not only his own dogs, but dogs owned by other hunters. Sire and dam breeding expenses as well as cost per puppy were determined by pedigrees and  standings and points earned at Field Trials. AKC said so. My Maggie and I did well in Derby Dog Trials and she became proficient in blind- and multiple-retrieves at a very young age. She was a gifted hunting dog and I was exceedingly lucky with our successes and lucky to hunt with her. She was smart, eager to please, and had a good nose. A hearty shout-out to Orin!

Butch's Molly was right behind Maggie. I talked Butch into also getting a dog from Orin. It was a milestone day when Butch's family met us at Orin's to pick out a puppy! My best friend and I would each have a black lab female to train and hunt with! Life did not get any better. What fun we had when on the way to Partridge Lake, for example, we would see a half dozen mallards in a pothole, coast on past, slip out of the station wagon, load the 12s, heal the dogs, blaze away, and send the dogs out on the retrieves! Then go hunting.

Gradually, I became part of Orin's dog training-hunting-social group. We frequented the Sports Shows in Madison and Milwaukee and other towns. He owned the Milwaukee Journal-Sentinel Sports Show until the newspapers bought it from him. The "Trout Pond" at the Sports Shows was a popular activity. Hundreds of trout were contained in a huge tank of circulating water. Dozens of patrons would pay a couple bucks to try and catch a trout using a furnished rod, line, and fly that was part of the package price. If they caught the largest trout for that particular Sports Show Season which ran usually for a week and two weekends, they won a trip to the Caribbean. There were daily prizes as well. I was told that a friend of mine who I met several years after it happened, who worked at the Milwaukee Public Museum, cheated and won the trip. Inside his pocket he had a small plastic bag. In the bag was a cotton ball that had anise oil on it. This guy would rent the fish rod, short line and wet fly and try to catch a trout. Before releasing the fly into the water, he would hold the fly up to the light, feigning inspection. Then he would smooth the fly out, using his fingers that were just rubbed with anise oil.

Orin and I, with George and his friend John who was also from Oconomowoc and ran for Lieutenant Governor and several others got involved in many other outdoor-oriented festivities. We also helped Orin in civic promotions like the Town of Eagle with "Eagle Days" which sported a parade, sanctioned dog races (mechanical rabbit), carnival midway, rides, etc. We had many good times and many good hunts. We shot pool, partied, hunted, and drank.

My first hunting trip to "Old Trail," Orin's deer camp near Boulder Junction, WI included Bill Hoeft, and Mel Ellis. They both were good friends of Orin and they both worked at the Milwaukee Journal-Sentinel. George, Orin's brother-in-law, did the cooking. A great man.

I was particularly honored to go with them because Orin and Bill and I had a weekly outdoor TV show entitled "Outdoor Reports." Bill wrote our scripts, Orin brought the animals and stories, and I was on camera.

Mel Ellis is one of my favorite authors of all times, like Aldo Leopold – a terribly gifted writer.

I told Mel that he personified what Anatole France said about authors: "the true mark of creative genius is to be able to write very simply about very complicated things." He modestly wrote back that he was no genius, "just a man of the land." Mr. Ellis wrote "Notes from Little Lakes" which was a regular syndicated column in the two Milwaukee papers as well as hundreds of other newspapers coast-to-coast. He also wrote books like <u>Run, Rainey Run</u> which won several journalism awards, <u>Wild Goose, Brother Goose</u> and many other award-winning books and stories. While we were deer hunting at "Old Trail," Mel got sick and Bill drove him back to Milwaukee. Bill was back at "Old Trail" for a pre-dawn breakfast! Probably a 450 mile roundtrip at least. Friends do that.

Mr. Ellis passed away a few years later. I wrote of my feelings to his wife, Gwen. Mel referred to Gwen as the "Rebel Queen" in his "Notes from Little Lakes" and his daughters as "Rebel I" and "Rebel II." Gwen sent me several of his books, some of which I did not have.

One deer drive at "Old Trail" was especially memorable. We were driving the edge of a swamp. A few of us were in the swamp and others were walking the edge. Orin was ahead of all of us up on the sidehill. A huge buck jumped up in the swamp and started running ahead of us. Suspecting it might dive into the swamp further, ahead of us (we couldn't see the deer), Orin took out a handgun and fired a "charge" over the deer which exploded on contact with the ground, out in front of the deer. The explosion turned the buck back to the high ground where Orin dropped it. It was fourteen points, eastern count. Another good friend of ours,

Bernie Gruenke, and I went out to Orin's in Eagle a few days later to see the hanging deer and take a few pictures in a snowstorm. Those pictures are some of my most artistic photographs and Bernie's wife had those very photos on display at Bernie's funeral in Milwaukee a few years ago.

Bud and I also hunted with the owner of the Boulder Beer Bar who was a deer guide. Wayne. We hunted with a bow when we were with Wayne. Sometimes, driving his pick-up, Bud in the middle and me with my bow on the passenger side, we coursed the side roads. In the early morning, Wayne would say, "See those three deer standing on the left side of the road about three hundred yards ahead?" I would get ready. Wayne would drive very slowly and while the truck was still moving, I would slide out the door, draw my bow, the truck would continue moving, the deer would continue to watch the truck.

One Friday afternoon I drove out to Orin's, which I often did on Friday afternoons before hunting seasons started. When I got out of the car Orin asked, "Don, do you have anything planned for tonight?" I told him I was going to be inducted into the Masonic Order, but that was not until later in the evening. He said to call my wife and tell her I would be a little late for supper, which I did. About an hour later we were in Freddy's Learjet (Miller Brewing Company) heading north from Milwaukee's Billy Mitchell Field. We stopped at the Duluth airport to check on a landing strip that was located over the border in Canada. The airport official said, "Well, it's a gravel surface, not too long, but you could try landing there." Freddy gave it a fly-over and minutes later we were in descent, in Canada, and I looked out the window. There was nothing but trees and lakes for as far as I could see in every direction. Orin had arranged to purchase a couple Timber Wolf pups, which was legal back then. We touched down, gravel flew, we stopped just short of the trees, got out, and about a half-mile away a rooster tail of water shot up from a lake. A rolling thunder (the sound of submerged dynamite exploding) swept across the land. A few minutes went by when two grizzled trappers came out of the woods carrying a cardboard muscatel box with two wolf pups in it. They wore heavy wool, plaid shirts on this very hot summer day. Back then, it was still legal to buy wolf pups from Canada and other wildlife, even bears. The trappers told us they were sorry to be late, but they were just fishing walleyes.

I asked the spokesman of the two trappers if he would let the pups out of the box so I could get some footage of them before the sun went down. He curtly responded, "Not before I get my money." While Orin peeled off a couple hundred-dollar bills, the other trapper asked me if I wanted to buy a couple bear cubs. I told him I did not really have a place for them, living in the City of Milwaukee, and politely declined. We talked a bit. Noticing he had a .22 caliber handgun on his hip, I asked if that was his defense when they went "cubbing" -- when he and his partner "bagged bear cubs." One of them would shoo the cubs up a tree, climb up after the cubs and stuff them, squealing, into burlap sacks. The other one would pester the mama bear. He said "Yah." When I asked him if he didn't think going up against a female bear with squalling cubs with only a .22 for protection was taking a chance, he replied, "Not for $100 it ain't taking much chance!"

Orin and his wife Lucille adopted a boy, Bobbie and a girl, Lynn who helped with feeding the animals and cleaning the kennels and cages. The Benson children had chores at the Game Farm and worked very hard. Kepa and Pake were a pair of Eastern Timber Wolves that Orin was keeping, in part for some veterinarians who were doing cataract eye research. The wolf eye is very much like the human eye. Jim Rieder in Franklin, WI also raised Timber Wolves and I was on Jim's Timber Wolf Foundation Board of Directors. While working at the Museum, I was in charge of arranging Wednesday Night Lectures throughout the several winter seasons that I worked at the Museum (1963-1972). These were primarily movie- or slide-illustrated lectures of approximately an hour in length, mostly travelogues. I had to plan the lectures in Spring. Since the Museum was the host of the annual series, I thought it might be a good idea to have a "Museum Omnibus Series" of lectures from the three local museums near Milwaukee. Therefore, I asked "Kip" Stevens of the Automotive (Excalibur) Museum in Port Washington, Jim Borman of the North Freedom "Railroad Museum," and Jim Rieder of the "Wolf Museum" in Greenfield to each present to our audience their messages and illustrations about their respective museums. Jim also brought his wolves on stage at the Schlitz Audubon Center for Saturday matinees to teach people about the wolves when I worked at the Schlitz Audubon Center (1972-1980). He could control his wolves, but said the wolves are never domesticated, nor would he let them off the leash or be further than arm's length. He gave me a marvelous opportunity to film one of his wolves running free along the beach at the Center, with neither leash nor collar. A very rare exception for Jim and the wolves!

When I was working at the Museum, I conducted workshops for youth. One of my workshops was casting animal tracks. I put some taxidermy clay outside Kepa and Pake's kennel at Orin's so when they came out to feed for example, they would push their paw print into the clay. My class members would then make plaster casts of the wolf footprints. When Lucille passed away, Orin remarried a lady who worked many years for the Wisconsin DNR, then she and Orin both passed away. Before he died, Orin asked me to write his biography. He had boxes and decade's worth of materials – mostly articles and photos from newspapers.

He wanted me to drive down to a nursing home where he was living and get from him these materials from him. He asked if I would go over the photos, articles, and other memorabilia with him, then write the book. At the time, probably 10-15 years ago, I told Orin that honored as I was to be asked, I did not have either the time or talent for such a milestone project. He seemed disappointed and died shortly thereafter. I regret not at least attempting the biography of such a good friend and well-known man.

Our "Museum family" was quite close-knit. We coffee-breaked, socialized, lunched, partied, hunted and shot trap and skeet together. Formerly located in the majestic Milwaukee Public Library building before moving across the street to the new multi-million-dollar Milwaukee Public Museum building in 1963, we took advantage of the used book sales at the Milwaukee Public Library because of our familiarity and proximity. Ken bought a used book entitled <u>Algonquin,</u> written by Dion Henderson. Ken got it for a dime. I was totally captivated by the author and the story and doubled Ken's investment, buying it from him for twenty cents. On the fly leaf, it said Mr. Henderson worked for the Associated Press. I called AP at their home office in Washington, D. C. and asked if I might be able to talk with Dion Henderson. Mentioning that I was calling from the Milwaukee Public Museum, the receptionist said, "Mr. Henderson works in our Milwaukee office, which I believe is right across the street from your Museum." Indeed it was. I called Mr. Henderson's Milwaukee office because the D. C. lady was kind enough to give me his phone number. I asked Mr. Henderson if I could take him to lunch. He agreed and asked if he could bring his secretary who he said I might also be interested in meeting. His secretary was Ernie Swift's daughter! Ernie wrote another of my favorite books, problems of the forties and fifties managing deer in Wisconsin. We had a fun-filled lunch, Dion preferred to be addressed as simply Don and Mr. Henderson signed my copy of <u>Algonquin.</u> I was ever so pleased to have met another famous author! My major "author regrets" are not having met Aldo Leopold or Wallace Byron Grange.

Old-timers at the Museum, mostly in Taxidermy, were often invited to Wallace and Hazel Grange's "Sandhill Crane Game Farm" in November before the opening day of Wisconsin's deer season. Wallace and Hazel had a section of land where they raised deer. They and their Museum friends would harvest the deer with jack lights at night. Most of the deer were served at high-end restaurants in Chicago and on the east coast. The Wisconsin Conservation Department finessed the Granges and the deer farm is now the "Sandhill Crane Wildlife Refuge" near Babcock, WI.

Come autumn, a few times the "gang" I worked with at the Museum -- Bill, Ken, Jim, Marv, Don, also Butch and George -- would stay Friday and Saturday nights at the Bluetop Motel outside of Fremont on Partridge Lake and hunt ducks. The Wolf River runs through an eastern corner of the lake. One time, for snacks, I brought a gallon pickle jar of roasted Woodcock breasts. Not many guys liked them. My dog, Maggie, did not even like to retrieve them. She would retrieve these birds, also called "timberdoodles," but only reluctantly. Maggie would curl her lips back so she would only touch a couple feathers with her teeth when bringing them to hand. It was quite comical to see a dog curl its lips back.

Herb and his brother Dick had a Citgo Station on Kinnickinnic Avenue in Bayview, south of downtown Milwaukee. Bud and Hans and Bobby, Dave, Herb and Dick were on the Citgo Trap Shooting Team #1. Since we were all good friends and hunted together, our Museum troupe accepted their invitation to put together Citgo Team #2 of Museum colleagues. Bill, Marv, Ken, Don, Jim, and Walter – from the tallest to the shortest. Bill thought it would be fun to have our picture taken in turn-of-the-century costumes. He went into the History Department costumes. The tallest guy, Bill, got the tallest stovepipe hat and the shortest blunderbuss gun; the shortest guy, Walter, got the most squat hat, but the longest gun. Very seldom did more than a couple guys break all twenty-five clays each week, but fun we had. We all pitched in ten dollars and Bill bought a reloading outfit so we could reload our own shells and save some money in his basement.

Several weekends, our Museum coterie stayed at my cousin Bob's cabin, the "Woodtick" near Iola. That was a quick-paced Ruffed Grouse weekend. Probably the favorite weekend of the year with  everyone who was lucky enough to be included. We did get birds. Some imbibing. And schopfskopf. Cousin Bob knew the land and had a good idea where the birds were. Bill brought his Brittany, KiKi who was a good scenting/pointing dog. My Maggie was a flusher but I held her close. When we got back after a day's hunt and close to the cabin, we would unload our guns and have the dogs at heel. Maggie and I were nearing the cabin one time and as I stepped over a hollow log that was laying across our path, Maggie dropped her head, picked up an adult rabbit that was in the hollow log, without skipping a beat. When we dry plucked and dressed the grouse, Bill would throw KiKi the head of one of the birds to eat as a "reward" for good hunting. I questioned that practice, thinking it might encourage your dog to eat instead of retrieve.

Bill was a very talented diorama artist and to this day, if you go to the Museum and view the major exhibits at the MPM, many of the backgrounds were painted by Bill. Or Ken. Bill also was the

International Decoy Carving Champion, often walking away with MOST of the international awards for ALL species of wildfowl carvings. Bill's son, Marc, is following is his father's footsteps. It is absolutely sensory-defying to see what Bill and Marc can do in wood! Bill once used a "curl" of wood from wood-planing a piece of pine to make a feather that floated on a pool of water (acrylic). By sight, you cannot tell it is not a feather! Ken also painted many outstanding backgrounds and murals at the museum. Jim became Director of Exhibits. Marv was the master head carpenter. He and his fellow carpenters built the underpinnings and super-structures, including a life-size colonial cabin at the Museum and the major foundations for the big displays. Walter and Harvey's "Buffalo Hunt" is a major work of achievement at the Museum. It is a life-size display of several Indians on horseback hunting buffaloes. I felt very privileged to watch the building of this exhibit from the mounting of the horses to the fashioning of the smallest leaf. This exhibit is truly a milestone marker for the skills of museologists. It is hard to imagine the talents necessary to complete such a three dimensional, life-size story of American history.

"With These Talents" is a feature-length documentary movie I produced on the building of the Tiger-Gaur Exhibit. I felt a need to record the skills that go into building such a masterpiece and was inspired, finally, after realizing what my friends were able to achieve in the "Buffalo Hunt."

A couple times for a weekend of hunting we stayed at Bill's father Henry's cottage in Wautoma and hunted the Princeton Marsh or Germania Marsh. The Princeton Marsh is laced with dikes and ditches. You pole or paddle your skiff in the ditches if you're trapping or hunting, then get out on a narrow strip of land – the dike. If you want to go further in, you pull your skiff across the dike, get back in and row or paddle to the next dike. This one Saturday morning, very early, Bill took Harvey who also worked in the Taxidermy Department of the Museum to the Princeton Marsh. Before dawn, a huge trapper named Bill Tate was two dikes out setting his muskrat traps. Bill and Harvey set out their decoys and waited for some ducks to fly over. And waited. And watched Bill Tate. Nothing flying. Finally, Bill S. thinks to himself, "I think I will have some fun with Harvey since he is here for the first time and since nothing is flying." Bill S. stands up and yells, "Hey, Tate, we're hunting over here!" Tate yells back, "I can see your hunting. I'm setting out my rat traps." About five minutes goes by. Bill S. stands up again, and through the cat tails yells to the monstrous Tate, "Will you get the hell off my water!" No formal reply. Tate just jams his pole into the bottom of the pond, picks his skiff up off the water by his feet lifting under the gunnels, swings the skiff in the air and poles the boat toward the dike that Bill S. and Harvey are on. There is a wake behind his skiff! Bill says to Harvey, "Oh, no! That's not who I thought it was!" And Bill pushes off the other side of the dike leaving Harvey to greet Tate! No place for Harvey to go! About the time Tate hits shore, Schultz yells, "Hi Tate, Bill Schultz here, having a little fun with you, my friend!" "Oh, Bill, I should have known." Harvey regained consciousness only moments later.

Another time, Bill and I were going to hunt Rush Lake northwest of Milwaukee on a Saturday morning to try to layout for some Redheads and Canvasbacks. At our Friday morning coffee break we told Harvey our plans and invited him along. He said, "No thanks, there haven't been any Reds or Cans on Rush Lake for ten years." The next Monday morning Bill flopped a plastic bag of Canvasback and Redhead heads on Harvey's desk up on the 6th floor in taxidermy and said, "How's that for no Canvasbacks and Redheads on Rush Lake?" After guffawing and reviewing the highlights of the Rush Lake hunt, Bill said, "See you at coffee break." Harvey said, "Leave the duck heads here, I can save you a trip to the incinerator in the basement, I'm going down to burn some old bird study skins." That was on a Monday morning. By Thursday, there was a decided aroma – more than vapors – floating around Bill's desk. His office was brand new. It was about thirty by fifty feet, "taxidermy-working-office" with a desk, tables each with a vise, a locker, a few storage cabinets and a polished terrazzo floor – quite clinical. By Friday, there was no mistaking it. Something was rotten or rotting. Bill scoured his office. The smell was strongest near his desk, which sat out in the middle of this cavernous, basically empty room. Not even draperies or curtains were hung yet in the brand-new Museum. Then there followed a warm weekend in October. Monday morning, the stench almost knocked Bill over when he unlocked the door to his office and entered! He suspected foul play by now and launched into the efforts of finding out what was causing such a stink. He even took the desk drawers out of his desk and put them back in. He removed the ventilator screens in the ceiling. Then he noticed something. Maggots on the floor. What was there a minute ago were his desk drawers. What? Harvey had nailed the duck heads to the backs of the wooden drawers in Bill's desk where they had rotted for about a week.

Sometimes we'd all sleep at my folk's house in Waupaca for a hunting weekend. Pop reminded me one morning about "Mary's Hill" on his rural mail route. Bill and I went out there and that was the first time ever that Bill "bagged out" with grouse. Five Ruffed Grouse in one morning!

One particularly memorable hunt on Partridge Lake was when I took my brothers David and Dale hunting with our Museum-friend Ken. Ken was another one of the very talented mural artists at the Milwaukee Public Museum. This particular weekend, Ken used Butch's skiff that I borrowed from Butch for the weekend. Butch had to work. He was hospital administrator at the Theda Clark Hospital in Neenah, WI. Brother Dale who was about twelve years old partnered with Ken. I rowed my skiff with David who was about fourteen and our skiff also had Maggie and the decoys. Both of our identical skiffs had oarlocks fitted to them for rowing across open water which was more efficient than paddling or poling. We started out long before there was any daylight. Joe Bell, Museum carpenter and good friend made the oarlocks for my skiff. The outside contour of the skiff met the deck at a ninety degree angle. That created a four-inch flat deck before rising another vertical four inches and the oval-shaped cowling. Joe sandwiched the four inches of flat deck between two pieces of white oak. The oak pieces, two on each side of the skiff, were held in place by stout bolts. He then augured two elliptical holes through the oak and fiberglass the same shape as the two prongs of the oarlocks, so the prongs would nestle in the holes, receiving the oarlocks. In the crook of the bend of the hardened steel oarlocks he welded a short length of pipe slightly larger than the oarlock pins. McGyver would have been proud of Joe for the job he did!

It was inky black when we put our guns, dog, decoys and gear into the skiffs. I notice Ken's anchor was hanging off the front of his skiff, over the water. That gave me a diabolical idea. While Ken was preoccupied loading the gear, I lowered his anchor a few inches so the anchor was skimming along the surface of the water. We boarded and started the mile or so from the Bluetop Motel landing, rowing across toward the northwest corner of Partridge Lake. What made this trip so special were two unforgettable experiences. One, brother David brought his harmonica. In the absolute darkness and stillness of the morning, with only the penetrating dots of stars above and the swish/swish of the oars, the tunes he played in time with the strokes of the rowing, were in keeping with the ethereal mood of the moment. A very special memory that we remember and discuss with fond feelings to this day. Also that day, David shot his first duck on the wing and I mounted it for him. A Bluebill. David was very proud. I was exceedingly happy for him.

Two, because Ken's anchor was skimming the water, the anchor and anchor rope were picking up the surface-floating weeds that coots had pulled up from the bottom of the very shallow lake over the last couple weeks. Ken was actually pushing a large mat or island of vegetation in front of his boat, but it was so dark he could not see it. He was pushing what I would imagine to be about 500 pounds of vegetation! Every once in awhile David would say, "How come Ken is slower than we are when Dale is lighter than

I am and we have Maggie? You must be a lot stronger than Ken." (Nothing is further from the truth.)

Butch and I relished floating the meandering Tomorrow (Waupaca) and Crystal Rivers. If Butch had to work, I would often borrow his skiff or hunt with someone else. And vice versa.

One weekend his brother John borrowed Butch's skiff, and I had already asked Ken to come to Waupaca for a weekend of hunting before ascertaining Butch's skiff was available. Butch told me he had to work Saturday, but John had never borrowed either of our skiffs before so it was an unusual happenstance. However, since Ken jumped at the chance to hunt and I could not disappoint him by bailing on him. We both hunted out of my skiff – only one gun loaded at a time. You shoot, then the other guy shoots – back and forth. Whether you got the duck or missed it if we were floating a river. In the morning, we hunted Partridge Lake. That night, Ken's shooting arm was black and blue from his neck to his elbow. He apparently did not cradle the butt of his stock in the crook of his shoulder, arm extended. That afternoon we had one of my favorite hunting experiences of all time and I have had lots of them.

Two hunters in one forty-pound, fourteen foot skiff. Ken weighed about 200 pounds and I weighed about 150. We put into the Tomorrow River at the Kennedy Farm west of town near the Bible Camp. Sometimes Butch and I floated this particular stretch of river, we would drop a few birds off at dam intervals, ostensibly so they wouldn't slosh around in the boat. One early Saturday morning when Butch and I were putting in at the Kennedy Farm, we spotted a little flock of nine Blue-Winged Teal swimming up the river right where we usually put the skiff into the river. Butch went one way around some bushes and I went around the other. Butch fired when the nine ducks were clustered in a little rapids between some rocks, swimming upstream, and got all nine of them with one shot.

Getting back to the story, on this particular Saturday when Ken and I put in at the Kennedy farm and got to the Cobbtown Bridge, mid-morning, which showed some white-water under it, Ken said, "Look ahead, whitewater!" I said, "Yeah. Do you want to carry the guns and camera around the rapids or shoot through the rapids alone in the skiff?" When we got a little closer Ken said, "You can't shoot through that water without tipping over!" I told him, fine. I would be happy to do it – "like my LITTLE brothers do" -- when they take the skiff on through the white-water. Ken said, "Really?" I told him to grab the guns and camera and I would meet him on the other side of the bridge. He said, "Hold on, if you and your brothers shoot this rapids, let me take the empty skiff through!"

It wasn't a real easy chute. It wasn't a "can't-make-a-mistake-chute". I told Ken what to do and how to do it. There was a big tree limb right in the middle of the whitest water that had to be negotiated. I told him to lay back in the skiff and <u>not</u> to lean to either side and <u>not</u> to grab the limb. He was doing okay when he got to the middle of the river above the bridge. I was set with my camera downstream. The first picture of the sequence of five pictures that I have of Ken is where he is entering the foam. His eyes are wide open. Like dinner plates. With eyes showing lots of white! The second picture is Ken approaching the tree limb, somewhat askew, not straight. Bad omen. Third photo is Ken grabbing the tree limb in spite of my admonition to "duck, don't grab or lean!" Fourth shot is Ken hanging from the limb in the middle of the rapids with the skiff about twenty feet downstream from him! The fifth shot is the skiff in the foreground of the photo, right at my feet on the river's edge with Ken obviously seeking help from the middle of the river, suspended on the branch from the big willow tree! It is a priceless sequence of photographs which has made the rounds because of the story it tells without words!

Another guy also named Ken lived across from our house on Wentworth Avenue. He was an avid, almost fanatical hunter. Ken told me about Bill's "Flam-Bow" Resort outside of Mercer, WI on the Chippewa Flowage. This Ken took me up there one autumn weekend. Bill, the owner, and I became close friends very quickly. We three hunted grouse. After that introduction to Bill and Marge and their resort, my good friend Bud and I went to the "Flam-Bow" numerous times. We went up there to bow hunt for bear and to fish for walleyes. Bill was a Wisconsin Department of Natural Resources licensed guide for hunting and fishing. Bud and I helped Bill and Mark, his nephew Mark, bait for bear a few times in the autumn just before season.

Bud and I went up to the "Flam-Bow" many times. Usually for hunting or fishing, sometimes to camp, sometimes with my family when we stayed in a cabin of Bill's. On the Fourth of July 1976, our country's 200th birthday, Bill said, "While the gals and kids get the picnic and fireworks ready, let's

throw some wood at muskies." I don't know about Bud, but I had never thrown a lure for a musky. Third cast: BANG! Forty-two pound, fifty-four inch musky! It now hangs in the lobby of the Flam-Bow Resort. That fish was the largest freshwater fish caught in America for about two weeks that year. Shortly after two weeks had transpired, someone caught a slightly larger musky in the Hudson River. We did get our pictures in the "Fin and Feather" magazine. I had the musky mounted for Bill by my friend Harvey at the Museum. It hangs in the lobby of the Flam-Bow Resort.

The only larger fish I ever caught was a sailfish out from Acapulco. Bud worked for an automotive chemical company in Milwaukee. Their company had a rule: when an officer went out of the country to deliver product, give a talk at a convention, or pitch a new automotive chemical product to company representatives, they were to be accompanied by another adult. Usually, another employee of the company was the other adult. Bud had to go to Mexico City. Nobody at the plant was available, so he asked if I would like to go with him. Naturally, I said yes. After his duties for the company were satisfied, we drove to Taxco and Acapulco. South of Mexico City, we stopped for dinner. There was a poster on the door of the supper club. It named a Don Danielson who was scheduled to fight a bull that evening. Not a coincidence as I thought at first. Bud's friend had set it up. Around a small bull ring, there were three levels of tables at this "Bull Fight Restaurant." The diners could look down at the bull and bull fighter. After a couple tequilas, I was convinced to "fight the bull." Decidedly a fun, dining experience for the local folks -- at the expense of gringos from north of the border who were "set up" by their friends.

The first thing I was taught, before the restaurant even opened, was to appear cool in the event of a charging bull. Then we went out back to the corral to pick out a bull. They looked big, mean and nasty. They pawed the ground and looked at us with blood in their eye. I am getting a little more than concerned at this point. What am I getting into? Given a cape, I was next shown how I could duck behind a solid oak bastion in the ring if I got gored or became a "chicken" after a charge of the bull. By now, I was ready to hide behind the oak wall before even seeing the bull. With a flourish of concertina music and cries of "Ole!" caroming off the three vertical levels ringed with dining tables and patrons who had filled the tables while I was getting directions on how to survive this bull fighting experience, I was introduced as the matador through the public address system. Thunderous applause, yells of accolades. By now, I have been escorted to the center of the ring and am trying to gain some composure. Evidently, this hoax was known to the diners, but not to the gringo participant. Out came a little black angus bull that was trained to butt whomever was in the ring! I put on a crowd-pleasing show of bravado, whilst still trembling within. After a tequila, picking up the flowers and wreaths that were thrown in appreciation, we left for the ruins of Taxco and deep sea fishing in Acapulco.

Deep sea fishing was not my cup-of-tea because the guide did all the work – baiting, letting the line out, et cetera. On "my" rod a sailfish struck, so I set the hook, and we boated  a nine foot ten inch sailfish. The skipper implied that I was stupid for not having the fish mounted because it was the biggest fish caught that season on his boat, the "Washington." Where would I hang a ten foot long sailfish? The only other salt-water fishing of which I have ever done was when Bud had to go to Daytona Beach. His good friend Howie was the distributor of their automotive chemicals down there in that part of Florida. We went sea trout fishing off New Smyrna Beach, near Cape Kennedy, and caught several fish. Howie grilled them right on his boat. Very tasty. That trip was when I got to drive a race car on the track at the Daytona 500 Speedway when we delivered automotive chemicals to the speedway and to Howie. I remember the track manager telling me to not go under sixty mph or the car would "fall off the track" on the curves!

Bernie Gruenke and I met at a Milwaukee Public Museum Open House – when the exhibit called "The Streets of Old Milwaukee" was opened to the public. 1964. Sy, sculptor in the Art Department, asked me to pose for the Native American featured in that first exhibit. My body is preserved life-size in clay! Radisson and Grossellier, fur-trader brothers-in-law who are suspected to be the first Europeans in the Milwaukee area back in the 1700s, are featured in the diorama with a Native American. One of the brothers-in-law has just shot a deer with a "thunder stick." Not having seen the bullet of course, the Indian is spell-bound and frightened by such "magic." That Indian is me, when I was skinny.

The Open House was an invitational, wine-cheese gathering honoring long-standing businesses who donated likenesses of their companies for the "Streets of Old Milwaukee." Bernie's family owned the Conrad Schmitt Stained Glass Studio which was an early industry in Milwaukee and one that was chosen to be featured in the Museum's "Streets of Old Milwaukee." Their stained-glass company has refurbished the Union Station in Chicago, the Union Station in St. Louis, and several large cathedrals in Europe, to name a few of their more prominent achievements. Bernie and I became very good friends. We would race our cars to Waupaca early, <u>come autumn</u>, to bow hunt for deer. The loser bought the Friday Night fish fry or first round at one of the local bars. I usually lost. It finally dawned on me that Bernie was not leaving downtown Milwaukee where his family's "Conrad Schmitt Stained Glass Studio" was located. He was departing Milwaukee about fifteen minutes closer to Waupaca than the Museum and Studio were located. He was leaving his home in Menomonee Falls where he lived. I told him that he could not leave his home until 5:15PM, to which he agreed, because I did not get off work until 5:00, downtown Milwaukee. The next Friday, I roared into my folk's driveway in Waupaca and right, I mean RIGHT behind me, comes Bernie! Like 200 yards difference after driving 120 miles! Trouble was, my Dad was on the front porch and saw the breakneck speedsters. For shame. At least I won. While guffawing and lording over my victory, I noticed a whitish "fan" on Bernie's turquoise Bel Air StaWag. The fan started at the passenger-side wing window and, widening out, eventually covering the whole right side of his car. I went over, swiped my finger through the fan – it was grease. Felt and smelled like animal grease. When I asked how that happened, Bernie said "While I was driving, Jim was grilling hamburgers on the floor of the front seat down in front of him with a Coleman stove!. The smoke was sucked out the wing window and apparently congealed on the side of the car." 100 mph. Open flame. No seatbelts. Wouldn't surprise me if both he and Jim drank out of a hose when they were young – maybe even rode in the back of pickup trucks without a seat belt.

Bernie was a non-conformist. That is a gross understatement. Once we were bow-hunting for deer and tenting about where my folks built their house on Whitetail Ridge, part of my great-grandfather's homestead just east of King, WI during bow season. The sheriff stuck his head in our tent around midnight – spotting a light in the tent where no light had been seen before -- when we were back from the Friday Night Fish Fry and a few games of pool. Sheriff Bonnell looked at us and said, "Donny, what are you doing with this long-haired weirdo?" Waupaca was not accustomed to seeing men with long hair back in the sixties. Long hair meant "hippie" to many people up north. Another time I hunted my grandfather's homestead where I picked blackberries with my grandmother and aunts when a little boy. This time I took Dr. Rick to Waupaca with me for a deer hunting weekend.

I hired Rick to be the Head Naturalist for the National Audubon Society's "Schlitz Audubon Nature Center" that we were building on the shores of Lake Michigan, nine miles north of downtown Milwaukee. I was hired as director of planning and programs and to staff and build the Center in the early seventies. Rick was the first staff member I hired and he and I founded Friends of the Schlitz Audubon Center to fund and support the Center's programs that were just getting off the ground. It became the first of the seventy-two National Audubon Society sanctuaries in America to become self-supporting. David R. and his family were the first official visitors to register in our Center's Guest book in early 1972 when the Center first opened to the public. David and I became good friends and pheasant and grouse hunting buddies. Matter-of-fact, some of the best wing shots I have ever hunted with worked for the Audubon Society.

Waupaca County was shotgun only for deer so Rick and I had our twelve gauges with slugs. We climbed trees that were about two hundred yards apart on the west end, late November, overlooking the Grand Army Home Cemetery in King, WI. There was a west wind, we were not protected from the wind, and Rick said he had never been so cold in his life. He must've been real cold because he spent a winter in Point Barrow, Alaska doing his doctoral degree research.

The following spring, I took Bernie to the Horicon Marsh Federal Wildlife Refuge. "Horicon" is a favorite stopover refuge for thousands of waterfowl, especially Canada Geese, both spring

and autumn on their two migrations each year. Some geese stay all year as long as the corn holds out. Another good friend, Bob Personius, was the federal manager of the Horicon Wildlife Refuge. He gave me keys to the dikes so I could take kids on school buses through the marsh on Museum Workshops in the spring of the year. I needed some audio tape sounds of geese gabbling for a documentary film I was producing for the Milwaukee Public Museum, so I took Bernie one spring morning to Horicon and we separated, each with a recording machine. Bernie was hunkered down about two rows into the tall corn in a food patch right in the heart of the refuge taping geese sounds. Along came a pickup truck, forest green, with U. S. Department of the Interior decals on the doors. One of the two wardens in the truck spotted Bernie, now hunched down even further in the corn, trying to escape being noticed. The truck came to an abrupt halt and the two guys popped out of the truck. Bernie said, "Hey, you guys! I found the perfect spot for my hunting blind!" They heard "hunting blind." Bernie meant "recording blind." We got it straightened out, eventually. Bernie was a jokester! He liked people and he liked having fun.

I maintained my friendships at the Milwaukee Public Museum during my gig with Audubon and continued producing movies.

Actually, I strongly believe that the decade I worked for the National Audubon Society was their "Golden Age." Their work with legislation, education, preservation, conservation, and general leadership in the environmental awareness movement would support that notion.

Harold was a guard at the Museum and an officer in the Wisconsin Society for Ornithology. We were camped one spring weekend at Crex Meadows in Burnett County, WI. On the Wisconsin-Minnesota border near Grantsburg, WI. Walking along a dike road, I heard the drumming of a Ruffed Grouse off to my left. Continuing my way back to our tent site, I now heard the drumming again. I triangulated the drumming, deducing they came from a little grove of trees about three hundred yards off the dike road. On a lark, I went over to where I thought the sounds came from. There was a log laying on the ground with some scuff or worn marks, smoothing the bark. After checking where the sun would be I late afternoon, I cleared a spot for my bird blind that would give the best exposure to a drumming Ruffed Grouse – should I be so lucky! About four o'clock, I went back to the site and set-up my bird blind which was approximately three and a half feet cubed with slots in the canvas for peering out and for my 16mm movie camera lenses. I had been in position for only about five minutes when this male Ruffed Grouse swaggers into view, hops up on the log and proceeds to drum. The drum sound is made by the bird breaking the sound barrier with its wings! That day, I recorded the best footage of a Ruffed Grouse ever! I also got footage at one hundred and twenty-six frames per second! This is super slow motion! It shows conclusively that the grouse, to attract a mate, does not stamp his feet like his cousins the Prairie Chicken or Sharptail, nor does he beat his wings on the log as once was thought. Matter-of-fact, although considerable energy and movement is obvious, the bird's head is absolutely motionless and fixed throughout the drumming which lasts about ten seconds, at half minute intervals, average!

On the top half of the kennel I built for Maggie at our house in Milwaukee (Bayview), I built a cage for our Minnie-the-Mouse. Maggie had the "lower suite" and Minnie had the "upper suite." Minnie was a female Great Horned Owl. One early March Saturday, Gil, Joachim, and I went "owling." The mama owls are on their nests and usually incubating eggs in late February or early March – our earliest avian nesters. I needed some 16mm movie footage of Great Horned Owls nests and climbed out on a limb that hung over a cliff to film this nest that had a couple tiny heads peering down at us.

Great Horned Owl nests are easy to spot in the spring. They are flat-topped, usually a Red-Tailed Hawk nest of the previous year, preempted by the early-nesting Great Horned Owl and often deserted and ready for the "owner/builder" female Red-Tail when she returns for her nesting in later spring. In this particular nest were three owlets. Two of them were getting their contour feathers. The other one was a downy, fluffy tiny chick that would fit in a teacup. Unlike the Ruffed Grouse females, the Great Horned Owl females apparently start incubating when they lay an egg. So subsequent eggs are incubated and therefore develop later than the earlier-laid egg(s). When I yelled down and described what the situation was, both friends agreed that I should bring the tiny one down, or the two older owlets would kill and eat it. So, I got my footage, stuffed the little girl owl in my shirt, lowered the camera gear down on the parachute cord, and with my climbing spikes descended the shagbark hickory. When I got down to the ground, I asked them what they planned to do with the little baby owl. They must have rehearsed their answer because it was delivered in unison, "What do you mean, WE? We each have an owl. This one is yours!"

So, I preempted the top of Maggie's kennel for the owl, which took a couple weeks because I am not handy with tools or mechanics. For two weeks we had Minnie in the house. Then she went out back into her "suite." Since there were so many rats and mice and rabbit remains ringing the outside of the nest we got Minnie from, like a wreath of rodents, I pilfered some of them and fed them in small but often quantities to our little owlet. My wife was not crazy about rats and mice in her refrigerator-freezer. A cage was borrowed from the Museum, approximately four feet cubed and that was her home for about two weeks. Minnie wanted to be fed every couple hours or so, but not lean meat only. She needed roughage also.

She grew rapidly. Each Monday I would take Minnie to work at the Museum. Minnie would ride on the top of the passenger front seat. Taking the freeway into town, drivers would look at Minnie and she would stare right back at them. I had built a nest of sticks on top of my file cabinet at my office window on the ground floor of the Museum. People would walk by each Monday, often with sandwich in hand around noon, to see her or see me weigh or measure her. Her nest in my office was constructed to look like her hatch nest. She would fly around the office, landing on books, fluttering papers, dropping "calling cards" and periodically pellets which she would eject after eating. Owls orally eject pellets, approximately one by three inches, tapered, after eating. Pellets are the nondigestible parts they ingest, like hair, toenails, fur, et cetera. When I felt that she was not getting enough roughage, like when I fed her lean beef or chicken, I would mix human hair with her food. We saved my son Mark's hair when my wife cut his hair, or mine.

One night my friend Gil who was now the director of the Racine Public Museum came to the door about 2AM. He was desperate for food for his owl and had been on the road for several hours. I gave him a frozen chicken breast and he bit off a big chunk, rolled it around in his mouth to soften and warm it, then tore off smaller chunks for his owl with whom he was traveling.

I will never forget a time Gil and I were visiting Joachim (Yogi) who was from Germany and an accomplished, licensed falconer. He had an owl also, as well as a gyrfalcon, and was being visited by a young boy who lived next door. The boy wanted to hold Yogi's owl on his arm. He was told not to quiver or move his arm once the bird was on his arm because the owl was trained to hang on to the perch. The youngster panicked when the bird's talons became a little tight. The boy tried to shake the owl off. The owl was trained to stay on. The talons went through the boy's arm, between the radius and tibia, and Yogi had to pith (kill) his pet owl to get the talons released.

One late winter, Yogi and I took my son Mark with us to try and capture a haggard falcon off Wisconsin Point, Lake Superior,

Moccasin Mike Road east of Superior, WI. We would sit in our respective blinds on the shore behind our noose-leg or catapult-spring traps with a pigeon nearby in a cage, which would attract the falcon to begin with. Mark wanted to chop wood because we all got pretty cold the night before in the tent. I told him he could chop wood, but he must stay on his knees and not rise to his feet while chopping. He complied (I could watch him down the shore about 500 yards) and that night we slept in warmth, thanks to my son who at the time was about seven years old.

Hunting seasons, my family and I or another friend and I usually went north to Waupaca. Or I would meet-up with Butch, or even stay at his place in Neenah. But not all weekends. Once our family went to my wife's folks in Holmen (LaCrosse), WI to see g'ma and g'pa. Her dad and I hunted the Black River for ducks. I had never before hunted from a boat anchored among tall trees near a heron rookery. It was good hunting for wood ducks and a few mallards. Other weekends, our museum clan and Bud went south of LaCrosse and hunted the Mississippi River for wildfowl out of Stoddard, WI. Many weekends I would hunt with museum colleagues – Bill, Ken, Marv, Bob, Jim. We were pretty tight and our hunting trips remain some of my best memories. Sometimes we would hunt nearby, west or northwest of Milwaukee. I recall one-time hunting ducks with Bill and Ken in a big marsh north of Lake Beulah. My knee went out and I had lots of ducks at sundown and could not walk without help. Ken was almost carrying me. We had a long way back to the car and it was getting dark. He mentioned that his load would be lighter "if we came back for the ducks tomorrow." Nope. Mink, weasels, muskrats.

It was quite late when we got to the car and Bill wondered what took us so long. Me. Sorry. That is a good example of how we felt about each other. He would not give me up even if I was too greedy for wanting to keep the ducks I shot.

Another time, Ken and I went out to Lake Beulah on a Friday evening after work. It was the first of the month. Ken said his uncle received his Social Security check on the first of the month and he always bought a case of beer when his check arrived. We drank some beers and went fishing. Ken caught a rough fish called a Bowfin, or Dogfish. He didn't know what it was. I just told him it was a Bowfin, but he didn't know anything about the fish and let the matter drop. When we got back to coffee break Monday morning, I told Bill and Jim about our experience with the Bowfin. Not one to let an opportunity slip away, Bill said, "Hey! We can have some fun with this!" Ken told the "Bowfin story" in which he was the star, so everyone knew he caught the fish.

Bill had been working on an exhibit at the Poynette State Game Farm Interpretive Center for the Wisconsin Department of Natural Resources. He had some official Wisconsin DNR letterhead stationery. Bill said he would give me a sheet of the letterhead, I would write a letter "pursuant to Section 111 of the Administrative Code of the Wisconsin Department of Natural Resources concerning Endangered Species ... "to Ken about this infraction. In the letter, Ken was admonished to call a Game Warden the next Friday evening between seven and nine o'clock in the evening for the arraignment time and date. Ken made the call at the appointed date and time. The Warden-role was being played by my cousin Bob, who was well appraised of what we were doing and Bob played along wonderfully when called him, right in the middle of a schopskopf card game! After hushing the guys who were guffawing at the card table, Bob said to Ken the court date was set for the following Thursday at the Federal Building which was across the courtyard from the Milwaukee Public Museum. Ken was quite distraught when he came to work on Monday. On Tuesday, Ken's wife called me, bawling because she thought the DNR was going to ban Ken from ever hunting or fishing again, in his life, and confiscate their house and car because both we used in committing the felony. Per the letter. (Remember, the Bowfin is a rough fish, totally unprotected, but Ken does not know that.)

Since this joke has pretty much run its course, we decided we should confess, but how?

Bill said, "For coffee break tomorrow, Wednesday, I will bring a folder with DNR letterhead stationery in it. Don, you ask me to sketch a 'Hunter's Pipe' decoy layout and I will bring out some letterhead paper, turn it over (after Ken has a chance to see the letterhead) and proceed to sketch the decoy layout. If Ken doesn't 'tumble,' we'll just tell him." Ken tumbled! He got red in the face, he stammered, the veins in his neck stood out, he broke out into a sweat, his pupils dilated, he blasphemed – all at the same time! It was beautiful!

One weekend everyone had something on their agenda except me. It didn't happen often. I asked my wife if she would take me and the skiff over to the shore opposite the breakwater at South Shore Park – she agreed. There was a strong, gale force, northwest wind (off shore), and I thought it would be a good time to get the Old Squaw ducks we needed for a Museum display. For a while,

I was the "hired gun" for the Museum – even shot ducks pretty much in the shadow of downtown's skyscrapers – because I had the Federal and State Collector's Permits. Milwaukee Chief of Police Brier would often watch me from a distance with binoculars when I was on a collecting expedition within the city limits. I rolled my skiff over in Partridge Lake once shooting a Baldpate for the Museum while leaning on the side of the skiff and ended up standing in "looncrap," but it was only three feet of warmish water. I did not realize how shallow that big lake was until I fell out of my skiff! Lake Michigan was different, more treacherous, especially with this wind. The wind was so strong, I paddled for all I was worth and barely caught the very end of the breakwater although I was aiming for the middle of the breakwater rocks when I started out! I was blown off course about a quarter mile in a 1000 yard stretch of Lake Michigan between the mainland and the breakwater. Needless to say, the wind was powerful. Had I not caught the end of the breakwater off Oklahoma Avenue, I would have been headed for Gary, Indiana. That is the closest I have come to real, life/death danger while hunting. A week or so later, I got the Old Squaws off the petroleum pier south of downtown. Two construction workers wanted to each bet me $20 that I would not get them. Another high wind, the birds were on the lee side of the long petroleum pier that jutted out into Lake Michigan, the pier was about twenty feet above the water, not conducive to an easy shot (no cover) nor an easy retrieve (wind blowing out and if shot, the birds would be twenty feet below me and who knows how far out). I walked the windward side of the pier until I figured I was just opposite the ducks. Then I got out my take-down spinning rod, laid it on the pier, loaded my side-by-side 12 gauge Beretta, crept across the pier, shot two Old Squaw ducks and retrieved them by casting and hooking them with my spinning rod.

After being chosen to be the first director of the Schlitz Audubon Center and leaving the Museum, we purchased a house and about ten acres about twenty miles north of Milwaukee on the Cedarburg Bog. Not only because their papa hunted were our three children used to eating game, but we also raised ducks and geese for the table (along with horses, sheep, etc.). We inherited with the purchase of our new house an inground swimming pool that we could not afford to refurbish. Our new house was north of Milwaukee – on the 3200 acre Cedarburg Bog. This is the southern-most "string bog" in the United States – characterized by vegetation growing predominantly at a right angle to the slight flow of water which flows northwest to southeast.

There used to be more species of wildfowl nesting in the bog, back in what we hear called "the good old days," and there are still several species that bring off their annual clutches. There used to be Giant Canada Geese (<u>Branta</u> <u>canadensis</u> <u>maxima</u>) nesting in the bog. I was told the Giant Canadas were nesting in the Cedarburg Bog as late as the late thirties. The University of Wisconsin Cedarburg Bog Wildlife Station was across the road from our house on Blue Goose Road and Paul, the manager, had good records on the bog and bird nestings.

Ilma Uihlein, grand matriarch of the Schlitz family and brewery and one of the kindest, most gracious ladies I have ever met, invited me to her farm, Afterglow, outside of Port Washington one late morning. At the time, I had left the MPM to direct operations as the director of the brand new National Audubon sanctuary on Lake Michigan that was to be called the Schlitz Audubon Nature Center. The Schlitz family and friends were exceedingly generous in funding this operation. It was to become a prototype outdoor learning facility on 200 acres of Lake Michigan shoreline. There are five major ecosystems on the property. It was an honor to be hired to direct the building, programs, trails, programs, staff, and operations of this marvelous facility. The Center has exponentially grown and matured since I was the first director (1972-1980).

I had an ulterior motive for wanting to visit with Mrs. Uihlein. Rumor said that she offered to sell her captive flock of about 200 Giant Canada Geese to Wisconsin DNR. They turned her down. She then offered the geese to the South Dakota Game, Fish, and Parks. SD was interested. I went out and had tea about eleven o'clock one morning with Mrs. Uihlein at her "Afterglow Farm" near Port Washington, east of Blue Goose Road. Following pleasantries and coffee I brought up the geese. She said they were going to SD, maybe ND, maybe it was Sand Lake Refuge. Whatever or wherever, I asked her if I could have about four pair for our place on the Cedarburg Bog. She said, "By all means."

You wouldn't believe her "accommodations" for her "babies." Her geese overwintered in roofed-over, heated pools (bathtubs) that were sunken in concrete, about ten geese to a pool. Plenty of food. No predators. Room to fly. Her hired man helped me catch four pairs that stuck together and we put them in gunny sacks.

I clipped one wing on each of the eight birds and put them in with my ducks, in the swimming pool, fenced overhead, from that autumn till the next spring. If you clip both wings, the birds can still get airborne, barely. If you pinion them (cut off the last joint on top of their wings), they cannot fly for the rest of their life. If you clip one wing, they can almost fly, but only in a circle. They quickly learn. More humane.

Our children were about ages ten (Maria), twelve (Marsha), and fourteen (Mark) at this time. They helped plant and weed and harvest a field of corn of about a half-acre each year in our backyard for their horse and their pony and for the ducks and geese. The birds became domesticated very quickly. In spring, they became "callers." How sweet to lie in bed and listen to them garble, then in the wee morning hours, start honking! In spring, they were also feisty and chased the kids around the yard because we let the birds out of the enclosure about the first of April. Our "callers" hearkened or called other geese down from wild birds in skeins going north. By summer, geese that had been netted and radio-collared or banded that morning for example in Horicon Marsh, were kibitzing at our place on Blue Goose Road with our geese in our yard and pond by noon! Bob Personius, Manager of the Horicon Federal Refuge was a close friend with whom I duck and grouse hunted, went decoy collecting with, and frequently I would call him and tell him I was going to send a bill to him because HIS geese were eating all MY geese feed. He laughed. One Sunday morning while we were getting ready for church, I looked down the driveway and saw about a dozen geese walking from Blue Goose Road up our driveway. Some of the geese had bands on their legs. Two of the geese had what looked like Coca-Cola cans on their necks! When I called Bob at the Refuge, he said that last evening they cannon-netted several geese and put red collars on some of them so the geese could be spotted more easily by hunters, maybe spared if hunters thought these collared geese were special.

Goose Fan Hopes Bog
Will Be Land of Giants

JANZ
at large

At the end of two years, Giant Canada Geese, like they did back in the thirties, were once again nesting in the Cedarburg Bog! There are Milwaukee newspaper articles about our "Giant Canada Goose Episode." They have been nesting in the bog, again, ever since Mrs. Uihlein's geese called to other geese from our place back in the late 1970's.

My son, brothers, and other friends and I have likewise had some exhilarating moments hunting near the Cedarburg Bog. When our family of five moved to the "Saukville Swamp" or "Cedarburg Bog" as it is also known, in the mid-seventies, it was a dream come true.

No city traffic on the way to work because I drove from rural Ozaukee County into northern Milwaukee County, at home we were surrounded by nature, my worksite was nature, my staff and I were engaged in the most purposeful work there is – educating people about the complexities and interrelationships of our earth and the need to safeguard them – as well as working with wonderful people with a similar passion for stewardship of our "spaceship" called Earth. And hunting right out the door of my home, front door or back door. One Sunday afternoon, the Packers were playing the Vikings in a play-off game. The football game went into overtime. I said to my family in the living room, "This is the last afternoon of the deer season and I still haven't hunted deer yet, so I will miss the overtime." I went out back, into the swamp and climbed a tree about two hundred yards from the house. About thirty minutes later, there was a shot. Maria told the family who were watching the football game, "I think I'll go out and help Papa drag in the deer," which she did.

Our son Mark and I duck hunted the open water of "the bog." He and I also hunted the surrounding farmland for deer. University of Wisconsin – Milwaukee owned part of the bog and used it for outdoor education. Mark and I also went to Wisconsin Rapids and hunted geese from the ritzy "Magnum Manor Waterfowl Hunt Club" thanks to my brother-in-law, Dick. My brothers came down and stayed in our "Bog Basement Man Cave" with the little wood stove (a house-warming gift from Dory when we hunted "the bog." One time when David and Dale came down to hunt deer, David had no sooner stepped into "the bog" (we wore boots) and a deer jumped up which he shot. Five minutes into the season!

When I resigned as director of the Schlitz Audubon Nature Center after eight years, ostensibly to finish my doctoral requirements in Educational Administration at Marquette University, which I did finish, we moved to northwestern Minnesota where I had my first school superintendent job – a little Norwegian hamlet called Gonvick. It is located between Bemidji and Thief River Falls. The morning we left Milwaukee, I was baptized into the Church of Jesus Christ of Latter-Day Saints in Lake Michigan. After my baptism, Phyllis my new wife, Jean, age seven, my new daughter, and I loaded up a big U-Haul truck and headed to Waupaca. My home town of Waupaca was on the way to northern Minnesota and that evening was my twenty-fifth high school reunion. I drove the truck and Phyllis drove the Datsun with Tippecanoe and Tyler II (the canoe and the skiff) on cartop carriers.

Tippecanoe was purchased from the Grumman Company in about 1964 and had seen almost as much float time as Tyler II our skiff. Tippi was more for family excursions into Horicon Marsh crooks and crannies, whereas Ty was mostly for hunting. When I found out that I qualified for the Outdoor Writer's Association wholesale purchases of writing and producing outdoor-related products, and thereby could buy a Grumman for cost, I did so. This was before we moved to the Cedarburg Bog.

I vividly remember painting the canoe with splotchy camouflage colors of marsh, gray, and brown so I could get closer to my nature subjects with camera gear without having to worry about tipping in a lighter weight skiff. The seventeen-foot Grumman was longer and much heavier than Tyler II. Back in the days when I was putting films together for the Milwaukee Public Museum, I used the Cine Special 16mm movie camera. With its compliment of lenses, filters, cans of one-hundred-foot film cannisters, protective cases, tripods and related gear, it was a heavy ensemble, maybe thirty pounds or more. The skiff would have been taxed – and tippy.

Up there in Gonvick, northwest Minnesota, for eight years as school superintendent, we mostly hunted the rice paddies for ducks and geese and the fields and woods for deer. Gonvick is a little

Norwegian hamlet and about ninety percent of the commercially grown wild rice comes from that area. Once I took my daughter Jean, duck hunting. I waded across a ditch in November to retrieve a teal to impress her to what lengths I would go to retrieve a downed bird. Jean was impressed, even at seven years old.

Maggie had passed away from liver cancer while I still lived on Blue Goose Road, so I did not have a retriever when we moved from Milwaukee to Gonvick. Phyllis bought me an eight-week old female, black Labrador pup soon after we arrived in Gonvick. We named her Cooper. She was coming along nicely at the age of about one year when I was in Harvey Erie's alfalfa field across the road training Cooper on blind retrieves. As she ranged back toward the houses, I blasted on my whistle because some knothead kid was screeching his tires around town and it sounded like he was coming down our road. Our one law enforcement officer, our "Chief of Police," was about twenty-one years old and was probably off duty at the time. Cooper heard the whistle. She was eager to comply and return to my side. Trouble was, the sound of the whistle bounced off the flat, reflecting sides of the houses and she ran straight for our house, away from me, and into the path of this hotrod kid who hit and killed her.

A Gonvick School Board member named Paul called me one spring afternoon. He had been picking morel mushrooms that morning. When he stooped to pick a morel, an explosion occurred at his feet. A female Ruffed Grouse catapulted off her virtually unseen and camouflaged nest of thirteen eggs. On average, a female grouse lays about an egg per day for approximately two weeks. Therefore, there is a lag of about two weeks between the first egg laid in the nest and the fourteenth egg. But the chicks all hatch approximately the same time! The reason for this phenomenon is that the chick embryo does not start developing within its shell until incubation begins. Incubation does not commence until the female has deposited the final egg of the clutch into her nest. When the chicks hatch, often within hours of each other, the little grouse immediately start scratching for food. Some bird chicks are precocial and are pretty self-sufficient as soon as they emerge from their captive shell – like the grouse chicks. Other baby birds are altricial, meaning they need considerable parental care and feeding for several weeks – like the Robin.

Paul knew that I was a wildlife photographer, so he called me and said he would take me to the location of the nest, which he did. After being introduced to Mrs. Grouse and her eggs, I went back to the site a few times. Each time I went back, she would let me get a little closer before flying, at first, then walking away from her nest. As luck would have it, the final time I went for a visit with camera in hand of course, the chicks had hatched and were cowering under Mom's wings. There were thirteen chicks. They

were all dry. The egg shells were most evident, but later the Mom would ingest many of them to replace the calcium it took from her body to produce the egg shells that encased the chicks during the twenty-some days of incubation.

The photo of the Mom and chicks is probably the best photo I have ever taken. I am proud to say it hangs in our friend's cabin on Elbow Lake, Orr, MN. Larry and Betty are wildlife enthusiasts and appreciate my photograph as much as anyone. Phyllis had the 35mm greatly enlarged and double matted to a large twenty-four by thirty-inch print – and framed. It is quite impressive in the story it tells without words.

Fellow church members and my new friends in Gonvick, Dale and Norm, and I did not hunt on Sundays, but we certainly hunted and fished lots on other days! I had been feeling a tad selfish for not spending more time with my new family, now a new wife and daughter, on weekends, so not hunting on the sabbath played into my plans. Northwestern Minnesota has some very good waterfowl hunting in the rice paddies. Having seen some unbelievably beautiful sights, I was especially amazed one late afternoon when Phyllis and I were driving the rice field roads. Off to the right of a flock of geese a flock of swans lifted off a paddy. They were backlighted by the low sun and framed by very dark clouds. I wished I had a camera. It was a most stunning scene! The scene reminded me of the waterfowl stamp that my friend, Marty Murk, fellow decoy carver who was also an artist, painted of Snow Geese flying past mounds of snow where the black tips of the Snow Geese wings where contrasted with snowbanks behind the geese and their white bodies were contrasted with navy blue clouds. He won the "duck stamp contest" with his rendition back in the nineteen sixties.

There was big water near Gonvick also. Not as big as Lake Agassiz that covered most of those states in prehistory times, but nevertheless big water. Norm the Third and his son Norm the Fourth and I went out duck hunting one windy autumn, cold day.

We threw out our "blocks" (decoys) and hunkered down in the blind made of rushes and cattails. The two Normans, father and son, had a sixteen-foot aluminum Lund and motor which transported us all with decoys, guns, dog, and lunches to our hunting spot. We towed my skiff for retrieving birds. After an hour or so with minimal action, I said that I was going to paddle my skiff around a bit, although it was exceedingly windy. About a half hour I came back to the blind. Norm IV said, "I heard a few shots. Did you get anything." I held up six mallards. About two hours later, I did the same thing. When I returned, son Norm IV asked the same question, "Did you get anything?" I said about a half dozen. I was coming back to the blind for lunch the second time when I paddled around the blind corner to a little bay. As soon as I swung the nose around to face into the bay, there were about a dozen mallards all hunkered together. They lifted off – obligated to fly toward me into the wind to get airborne -- as I shot my side-by-side twelve gauge, both barrels, and six more mallards became table fare. The ducks were in an unfavorable position, having to fly at me to get airborne, against the gale-force wind.

One Saturday, Papa Norm caught a huge Northern when we were fishing one of his favorite local lakes. Normally I have my camera, but it was left at school this particular weekend.

So, back to town we went. I had Norm sit in my school superintendent office chair at the school and took his picture. It is such an incongruous scene with muddy Norm at a beautiful desk in a well-ordered office, holding a slimy Northern in his hands. Lots of wildlife up there in northern Minnesota between Bemidji and Thief River Falls, good hunting and fishing. My church friend Steve, our best man at our wedding, worked at the rice paddies for a rice farmer. One day Steve was eating lunch out of his lunchbox, sitting on a dike, and a muskrat stuck his head in Steve's lunchbox! Steve does not share his lunch, so he killed the muskrat, put it in his now empty lunchbox, took it home, skinned it out and sold it after stretching it.

One time, Dale and his son Brad and I were hunting wildfowl on the paddies. Young Brad was driving Dale's pickup which had their camper on the back. Brad got a little too close to the edge of the very narrow dike and the truck started to slide down the embankment. Fortunately, Brad stopped before the truck hit the water. Now what? Twenty miles from town, our vehicle is mired. However, since Dale worked at this farm previously, he knew how to get into the machine shed that was about a mile away. We walked to the shed and were going to get the wild rice combine to pull out the truck. However, the battery was not in the combine. Back we went to the truck. Pulled the battery from Dale's truck, walked back to the combine shed, installed the battery in the combine and motored the combine back to the truck and pulled it out! How many people have pulled a truck stuck in the mud out with a wild rice combine?

It's not exactly a hunting story, but Dale's daughter Brenda shot a cow during hunting season. Now, don't jump to any conclusions. Brenda was in high school and was an excellent huntress herself. Their neighbors, way out in the country where they lived, had their livestock pasture surveyed. The edge of their neighbor's pasture was directly beneath Dale's eaves of his house. To ensure or cement good neighborly relations, the neighbor could have moved his electric fence, even just a yard. He would not do that, even for a fair sum of money and a resurvey for which Dale would pay. Several times, one or more of their uncooperative neighbor's cows would get out of the pasture and wander into Dale's yard, rooting up his wife RuthAnn and high school daughter Brenda's gardens. Brenda, usually it was Brenda, would dutifully grab the halter and take the cow back to its rightful owner. One time, after numerous infractions, she told the neighboring farmer, "The next time one of your heifers comes into my garden, I will shoot it." About a week later, the cow did and Brenda did. Dale dragged the carcass over to the front lawn of the neighbor with his four-wheel drive truck. Nothing was ever said about the incident that I know of.

Dale had the outdoor toys. Snowmobiles, boats, motors, parasails, guns, fishing equipment, you name it. He was a master in their use and maintenance. When he took us parasailing on Clearwater Lake, I looked **down** into an eagle's nest! Dale was about 200-300 feet offshore with the parasail attached to the cord that is also attached to the boat. He guns the motor and I ran toward the water until I became airborne! It reminded me of when Bud and I went to Mexico. In Acapulco, I parasailed with my camera which was not supposed to happen. The reason the camera was not detected, I think, is because I had the strap around my neck with the camera on my back so the camera was not visible or obvious. I did not know it was illegal to take a camera airborne. What surprised me was the belly of the towing rope when you are so many hundred feet above and behind the boat. I thought the rope would be more straight between the boat and the person in the air, but there is a pronounced belly in the rope. In Acapulco, you were always over deep water. With Dale, you could steer your sail and go over land if the boat was near shore. No restrictions. That's when I steered over a big White Pine and looked down into the eagle's nest.

After about four or five years in Gonvick, I had shot about one deer each year. One time, hunting deer with Dale near Pine Lake west of town, I was stalking the cedars and came upon a grouse. It was on a log not far away, maybe forty feet. Knowing that the grouse season was still open and figuring the difference in trajectory and line-of-sight through the scope, I de-capped the grouse. I put the deer racks on our outside, shelf bird feeder so the birds could perch on the tines and beams while waiting for their chance to dine. Right outside the dining room window. Few expenditures than sunflower and Niger Thistle seed have given us more pleasure than watching birds come to the feeders all winter long. That is true wherever we lived. There was quite the variety of perch options for the finches, grosbeaks, nuthatches (both White-Breasted and Red-Breasted), chickadees, woodpeckers and others on the deer antlers.

Dale had lived in northwestern Minnesota all his life and was familiar with just about all the hunting and fishing options around. He took me to a little crossroads called Four Town, which was several miles north and west of Gonvick. Since we had birds in our own area, I thought Four Town must really have birds. It did. When we hunted there, quite a bit of snow had accumulated and I wish I had brought snowshoes. We got birds and when my son John came to visit us the next winter, I took him to Four Town. John said, "I think I will poke out this swamp for an hour or so and come back this way." I knew he would return because the swamp became wetter than he had boots for in about a half mile – he had to turn back and return. When he got back to where we parted, I had built a fire and roasted a grouse on a crude spit. We sat down and devoured it! John said, "I've never tasted anything so delicious!" It's funny that food tastes so much better in natural surroundings.

Across the road from our house, on the very edge of Gonvick, was Erie's farm. I trained Cooper in Harvey Erie's alfalfa field and hunted his woodlots for grouse. Jean rode her Welch pony in their creek and woods, except during hunting season. He worked at the Post Office and she was on the Gonvick School Board. Good people.

Church friends, David and Helen, bought a yacht. They pretty much put Dale in charge of their boat. We spent great times on the yacht on the huge Lake-of-the-Woods (LOW) in northwestern Minnesota because we lived pretty close to this watery, island-studded natural paradise. There were several lodges at the entrance to LOW that we stayed at when we did not go on the Dickey's yacht and when family members like Phyllis' folks came for a visit, as did my Mom and other relatives. LOW had thousands of islands and great walleye and eelpout fishing.

Phyllis and I went walleye fishing with David and Helen and "the kids" of our three families one particular weekend. We took Phyllis and a couple of the kids who felt the call of nature to a little island. Among their activities while we waited on the boat for them, Phyllis inadvertently dropped her favorite sheath knife in the bushes. She still had the sheath when we returned home, but no knife.

On the same trip, Dale's son Brad was about sixteen years old and a most accomplished fisherman. He put a leech on his line and we were trolling for walleyes – and catching them. Something didn't feel right, so Brad reeled in. His leech had sucked-on to a tiny walleye! Like in "Man bites dog," "Leech catches fish." I have a picture of Brad proudly holding up his trophy.

About two weeks later, the adults of the families were yachting for walleyes on LOW. Phyllis and I had been selected to go with the kids, so the Dickeys and Crepeaus went this time, just the four of them. The boat comfortably slept six, but the kids needed a chaperone and we were chosen by the kids to go with them and that meant we opted out of the "adult weekend." Anyway, RuthAnn gets nature's call, so they motor to a small island. None of the occupants on the boat this particular weekend were occupants on the boat when Phyllis lost her knife. Imagine our surprise when the following week at church, RuthAnn says to Phyllis, "Look at this charming knife I found on a tiny island up at LOW!" Later, at a "Wild Game Dinner Party" at our Church of Jesus Christ of

Latter-Day Saints, Phyllis thanked RuthAnn again and showed her the knife back in its familiar sheath.

Our wild game dinners at our Church of Jesus Christ of Latter-Day Saints were legendary! We men did them – our Elder's Quorum. We hung nets, traps, guns, pictures and things like mounted deer heads and fish on the walls. We dressed in camouflage and many of us even painted our faces with brown and green. Phyllis invited a non-member of the Church to the party and told her that dessert was going to be chocolate mousse. She almost didn't come to the party because she thought it was chocolate moose. We had all kinds of game, roasted, baked, cooked, broiled, grilled all kinds of ways.

The first deer I shot in Gonvick was on Dickey's farm, hunting with Dale. Dickeys were also members of the Church of Jesus Christ of Latter-Day Saints. I bought a tree stand, but still needed to climb a tree to fasten the stand securely to the trunk – which I did about a week before season. Opening morning I climbed up, got situated, remained motionless with my eyes wandering in the direction where I thought might come the action. About ten o'clock an eight point was pussy-footing along, from the direction Dale was posted and I was concentrating . I wondered why Dale hadn't shot it, but apparently the deer veered off when approaching his stand and it didn't come close to him. Dale missed nothing when it came to hunting. I shot the deer and about ten minutes later Dale came over and called across a swale, "Did you shoot?" I replied that I had and if he took a few more steps toward me, he would find the deer, which he did. He probably came over to help me track it. Another time, after Dickeys had sold the farm to the

Clay family, I asked Jean who was about twelve or fourteen years old if she would like to go deer hunting with me. She said no. She had gone duck hunting with me, so I thought maybe she would like to see what deer hunting was like. Later she said, "Where are you going deer hunting?" I told her Dale and I were going to hunt the old Dickey farm. Jean said, "Isn't that now owned by the new family that moved in? The Clays?" I said it was the same. Jean was interested in their son who was a year or two older than she. Jean reconsidered and I put her in a tree about a hundred yards behind me where she could see my back and what was in front of me, a big field. In the middle of the field, about two hundred yards out, was a lone bush about three feet high. It was important to me to know that distance, so I paced it off a day or two previously. About shooting time, I looked out in the very subdued light of early morning and saw two bushes! Looking through my binoculars, one was a deer. The deer also had branches! Boom! Eight-point buck.

Over thirty years ago when we moved to South Dakota from Minnesota, Norm bought my cherished, twenty-year old skiff for $100. About a week ago, December 2018, Norm's son Luke told me he is using the skiff for duck hunting and it is stored at his hunting buddy's place in Grygla, MN. There is no vestige of hunting paraphernalia that has brought so much

happiness and joy so deeply entrenched to its owner than Tyler II – my cherished skiff. I can only hope it brings the same to Luke whose father is in a nursing home with Alzheimer's Disease. I wonder if Norm can remember the good times we had hunting and fishing. Most sincerely, I truly hope he can.

After eight years in Gonvick MN, we moved to Redfield, South Dakota where I was school superintendent of a larger school. Redfield is the capital of Spink County, about fifty miles south of Aberdeen and seventy-five miles west of Minnesota in the northeastern part of the state. It is well known for being the place where pheasants were first successfully introduced into the United States. With gun in hand and glint in eye, the "pheasant factor" lured me to apply for the job – with about forty other applicants.

I fully admit that the best hunting and fishing I have experienced has been in South Dakota. Quail hunting in Illinois was good. Duck and deer hunting in Wisconsin was good. Grouse and deer hunting in Minnesota was good. Generally speaking, however, the

best hunting and fishing I have had has been in South Dakota. Not so much grouse, but deer, ducks, geese, prairie dogs and fishing.

My Viet Nam sniper buddy, Mike, who owned the bakery, was in charge of the Ducks Unlimited Banquet each year in Redfield. Since I helped with the DU Banquets in Milwaukee, I asked Mike if I could help with the auction items. Local businesses donate hunting-related gear which is auctioned off to the highest bidder. The next spring, most of the money goes to purchase pheasant chicks that are raised by the local landowners and released just before hunting season.

My friend Dave who was the first Schlitz Audubon Center visitor almost twenty years ago and I kept in contact. Dave came to Redfield to hunt pheasants. He arrived the day of the DU Banquet and stayed with us for a few days during which time Mike guided us to pheasants. At the Banquet, while Mike and I were hawking the auction items, Dave bought a complete set of Duck Stamps that was matted and framed. Dave owned the Northwestern Mutual Life Insurance Office of about sixty representatives in Madison, WI by now and the famed and framed "Duck Stamps" became and integral part of Dave's office décor.

Our daughter Jean was a junior in high school when we moved to Redfield, SD. The K-12 public school had about a thousand children. It was the only school I had ever heard of that had fresh-baked bread and rolls on the hot lunch menu every day. Mike Lee owned the Bread Box Bakery on Main Street, downtown Redfield and had the contract to supply the school with bread and rolls. He and I became very good friends quickly – are to this day some forty years later. Mentioned previously, Mike was an Army sniper in Viet Nam. Although I knew Mike for years before he told me any stories about his military role in 'Nam, we became fast friends.

The first time we hunted ducks together, neither of us knew the hunting orientation of the other. We were sitting in a corner fence row on a little river bank with stalks and weeds pulled over us to obscure our location from ducks flying overhead. We marveled at the number ducks that were dropping into a bend in the river about three hundred yards upstream, but none were venturing downriver as far as we were. Finally, Mike said, "Do you want to sneak up on those ducks?" I replied that we had to cross the river to stay out of sight and neither one of us had boots. He offered to take me across the river piggy-back – that's the kind of guy he is!

I told him I would stay where I was and get a couple stragglers when he spooked the ducks.

I believe I did get one mallard.

Mike crawled about three hundred yards, after wading the river, while keeping his black lab female at sit until he called her after crawling about fifty feet. Then he would have her sit again and crawl another fifty feet. By Mike's behavior, I could tell he was getting close to shooting distance. He stood up, fired two times, and the skyline was peppered with black dots called ducks. I walked the shoreline down to the ducks – coming in view of the bend in which the ducks were congregated soon after leaving my blind which didn't matter now that the ducks were gone. We had the dogs retrieve twenty-two mallards that Mike shot with two rounds! After driving to Redfield for lunch, we went back to the same spot and Lady, his lab, found two more dead ducks. When I asked him why he only shot twice he said his gun was legally plugged (two shot maximum when duck hunting). Also, he could claim he got one duck with the first shot and twenty-three dropped with his second shot if challenged which would be plausible as well as legal.

Mike and I had Black Labrador, female, litter mate sisters. His was named Lady. Mine was Cede (Sadie), which was short for Mercedes cum Laude.

My sister, Deborah knew Cooper was buried back in Gonvick on the Bardwell property where we had poked around for grouse – Cooper and me – and that I was without a dog, Debbie brought two eight week pups to Gonvick. I thanked her for doing so and picked one of the pups. I told her hat Mike might want the other one. Mike was golfing out at Fischer's Grove Golf Course east of Redfield, so said Deb, Mike's wife when I called their house. So, I boxed up the pup that became named Lady and drove out to the golf course. Mike definitely wanted the pup and I took the pup back to their house where Deb wrote a check to my sister's friend who raised retrievers. We trained our pups to blind retrieves and hand-signals. They had good noses. We hunted pheasants innumerable times and ducks almost as much. For years.

Mike and I golfed lots too. One summer we figured we golfed approximately 2000 holes. One day we left the bakery about sun-up, golfed eighty holes, and came home in the dark after the golf cart broke down on the eighty-first (ninth, nine round hole). Summer golf turned to, **come autumn**, hunting. Mike would start baking about 3:00AM and I would get to the bakery about 5:00AM. He called me his "fry baby" because I flipped the donuts and glazed the raised donuts and the apple fritters. For almost forty years I have compared apple fritters around the country to Mike's Bread Box Bakery fritters and have found none as good. Mike used fresh apples and cinnamon from Madagascar, I think he said.

The potholes we hunted for ducks in South Dakota had more

gadwalls and pintails than we had in either Michigan, Wisconsin, or Minnesota. Other duck species too and thousands of Snow Geese and "checkerbellies" but not as many Canadas. Our family, thanks to Mike guiding, continued to eat wild game. Venison, pheasants, deer, and ducks mostly. As one might expect, Mike was a superlative marksman. One time when he took his niece Jennifer deer hunting, they were in his truck and a deer was about four hundred yards out. Jennifer asked her G'Pa why he didn't shoot the deer and Mike said he would prefer a closer shot with the caliber he was carrying. After a couple minutes of watching the deer watch them, Jennifer picked up Mike's auto-focus binoculars, got the deer in view, and exclaimed, "Shoot now, G'Pa! It's lots closer!"

Recently, Mike bought a Finnish-made Lapua .238 caliber for competitive shooting. He is able to put five shots in a six inch pie plate at 1,000 yards! He times his shot between breaths and heart beats.

Out in the flatlands of South Dakota, potholes are sometimes a long-ways apart, but Mike knew the country. He had been scouring the land and making friends with farmers who owned the best hunting land around Redfield for about thirty years before I moved to town. I had not hunted pheasants that much when I came to South Dakota. One particularly gusty, blizzardy day, we were driving a section line road and Mike said, "They'll be in the trees today." When I started looking up in the trees, Mike said, "Not up in the trees, but in the tree lines and brush lines for protection from the wind and snow." I felt quite foolish because I should've figured.

I got fired after a few years because the Redfield School Board "lost confidence" in me. Three of the five School Board Members had three-year old children, daycare was expensive, and if the Redfield School District would institute a Three Year Old Kindergarten, they would have their children cared for in a learning environment by certified instructors. Paid for by the school district taxpayers. I thought about it, corresponded and consulted with kindergarten experts across the country and with leading and the local teacher-training colleges in South Dakota and the Midwest. Nobody in the field of education could find "any significant difference" comparing young adults who had gone to three, four, or five-year old kindergartens, so I recommended we not take on another two years of toddler education expenses (to provide babysitting for the three Board members). As a result of my decision, they "lost confidence in me" and I hit the road by popular demand.

Right away, I was found a job as school superintendent in Minong, WI between the Gordon Flowage and the Minong Flowage. Good duck hunting and good grouse hunting and good deer hunting.

We bought a mostly finished house on Miles Lake, about four miles northwest of town. We were the only year 'round resident on the lake. Instrumental in making our decision to buy the house was an enormous White Pine with two eagles in it when we first visited the site. Since Lady Phyllis and I met counting Bald Eagles in Alaska we regarded this sighting of eagles as a good omen. Turned out to be a good omen after we bought the property. Mike came over from South Dakota several times, bought a johnboat from Bob Link in downtown Minong, and we fished Miles Lake quite often for a couple years.

Dave, my friend from the Schlitz Audubon Center who was on the Board of Directors at the Center (who visited us In South Dakota and bought the Duck Stamp Collection), called and asked if I would like to join their party of three grouse hunters and stay a couple days in the condo that he and Eileen bought at the base of the Powderhorn Mountain Ski Slopes at Ironwood, northern Wisconsin. "… and Don, please bring Cede." I was teamed up with a dentist friend also from Madison, WI. His name was Dr. Grimm and he was the fifth great grand-nephew of the two Grimm Brothers who wrote <u>Grimm's Fairy Tales</u>. Between searches and shots for and at grouse and woodcock, I learned the story of the Fairy Tales. The two Grimm brothers were bachelors who lived together since their youth. When the Grimm Family had a gathering or reunion, when the table was being cleaned and the dishes washed, the two brothers would get the kids around the fireplace, for example, and tell stories. Later, a member of the family compiled the stories, bound them, and called them <u>Grimm's Fairy Tales</u>.

Bob Link, famous Minong resident for having the largest Mercury boat motor sales floor in Wisconsin, as well as the largest aluminum boat sales floor in the Midwest, grew up on Miles Lake in the cabin that was deserted and right next to our house. One day I was standing on a couple pallets that we called our "dock" and Bob Link came paddling by in an inflatable boat that he was trying out to determine if he wanted to carry the line. I yelled, "Bob, what do you think you are doing on my lake?" He chuckled, came ashore and we talked while sitting on the deck of our new sauna that I just put in. After a while, I asked, "Bob, do you ever trade for boats, canoes, motors, and trailers?" He confessed that he hadn't done much of that, but he wouldn't rule anything out. I told him that I would trade my Grumman canoe (getting too heavy for me to portage even though I went to the BWCA frequently) and some wildlife prints and American stamps for a new lightweight, fiberglass Penobscot canoe; six horse motor; johnboat; and trailer. He said, "Well, let me think about it." Probably a couple weeks went by. We met uptown. He said, "Why don't you come over to my store, pick out the stuff you want, then lay out in your living room the things you would give me? Let me know the day you have the things you would trade laid out and I will pay you a visit. I'll know the cost of what you want, will try to figure the value of what you would give me, and we'll talk."

From working at the Milwaukee Public Museum and for the National Audubon Society, I had some Audubon wildlife prints and calendars and a stamp collection of plate blocks that went back to 1972 – every stamp produced by our Postal Service from 1972-2002 except the high-dollar ones. Plus my Grumman. We shook hands on the deal. I felt a pang of nostalgia when I parted with Tippi. I originally got Tippi to produce, "Way of the Wilderness" which was a hour-long documentary, full length feature movie for the Milwaukee Public Museum on the Boundary Waters Canoe Area in 1965. Tippi was a member of the family. I also used Tippi for other illustrated lecture films that I presented to groups in Milwaukee under the auspices of the Museum. Lectures on Great

Horned Owls, Ruffed Grouse, Ospreys, Bald Eagles, Isle Royale, and Camping With a Naturalist.

Tippi's maiden voyage was the Sylvania Wilderness and Porcupine Mountain area of the Upper Peninsula. My, wife, our three children, Maggie our twelve week old female Black Lab that I got from Orin, all our camping gear and food for a week, and a case of beer. Bob and Rita had the same complement – three children, gear and food, dog, and another case of beer. The major good that came out of our venture was catching a twenty-two inch Smallmouth Bass and building family memories. Our little pup was plagued by black flies and biting houseflies. We caught the hatch. Little Maggie burrowed into the soil at the entrance but under our tent. Only her nose stuck out of the earth. As young as she was, she instinctively knew what to do to escape the bites of the black flies!

Now, thirty years later, after trading with Bob Link, we surely liked our new sixteen foot, fiberglass Penobscot canoe; our new six horsepower motor; new fourteen foot johnboat (now Mike did not have to bring his from South Dakota when he came over to fish Miles Lake with me); and our new boat trailer. We were set.

There was a small lake directly across Miles Lake, but separated from Miles Lake by a strip of land about sixty feet wide. Son John and I set out decoys for ducks on a couple occasions when the wind was strong on Miles Lake, but we did not get many ducks or shots at ducks.

I remember butchering deer, cleaning ducks, potting wildflowers to transplant on a four-by-four piece of plywood. The same piece of plywood was used as a door to a snow fort that my brother Darren and son-in-law Dan and I built – complete with shelves for candles and Jack Link jerky. The same piece of plywood was used for a ramp to jump Dan's four-wheeler on frozen Miles Lake and for "ditch skiing" behind a car after a big snowfall. The same piece of plywood was pulled behind our johnboat on Miles Lake after we upgraded to a twenty-five horse boat motor. I put a two-by-two inch "keel" on the bottom of the plywood, so it was fairly good tracking behind the boat as we stood on our heads on the plywood, sat on a chair while "plywooding," and did other crazy stunts for the amusement of family and neighbors. When we moved from Minong, my brother Darren helped us load the trailers. Speaking of nostalgic moments, we both were sad to burn our "plybaby" since the trailer was full to overflowing.

There was not much of a choice, moving from Minong. I was encouraged by patrons and felt personally compelled to investigate an illicit relationship between a school employee and the School Board President. The president told me that if I bring the matter up, he would fire me. The common knowledge of this affair could not be allowed to go on, so I started making inquiries. I was fired. People in town found out why I was fired, had a spring election, and voted me onto the Minong School Board to replace the president who moved his family to California. By the time of the special School Board election, I had gone canoeing in the BWCA with my brother Darren and his boss Seth who ran IDS Financial Advisors in Duluth. Seth asked me to get licensed and become a financial advisor. I took the tests and got my Series 7 and 63 and gave it a whirl for about four years (1994-1998). Didn't do well at it. Didn't like it. We moved to Granton when I found another school superintendent's job. A couple nights before we packed-up to move, I felt a mouse run across my arm while lying in bed. Maybe I was imagining things. Then I heard a little thump, thump and turned on the bedside lamp in time to see the mouse trying to jump from the dresser to the ledge of a picture frame. It finally caught hold and pulled itself up. When I got out of bed, the mouse jumped down on the dresser, then jumped down on the floor. The dresser was about an inch from the wall due to the molding and the mouse was sitting on the floor molding. I got a flashlight and pellet gun, held the flashlight in one hand and the pellet gun in the other. Squeezed, dead mouse. Duct tape on a yardstick for retrieving the mouse. When we moved the dresser out to load it on the U-Haul when we moved about a year later, there was one little fleck of mouse blood on the white molding. To this day, my wife thanks me for saving her life! Her own "Big Game Hunter!"

There was not "blood in my eye" when I accepted a school superintendent job in Granton, WI.

We did some canoeing, but I did not hunt much anymore. Matter-of-fact, we had turkeys and pheasants and grouse and deer on our own property, and we still had Cede, but I was rereading books that I had read in years past like Aldo Leopold's "Sand County Almanac" and "Game Management," Mel Ellis' "Notes from Little Lakes" and "Run, Rainey Run," and "Wild Goose Brother Goose," Susan Flader's "Thinking Like a Mountain," and other authors like Fred and Frances Hamerstrom, Ernie Swift, Rolf and Candi Peterson, and others who wrote more of a land ethic than a hunting ethic – both of which I feel are critical to our inner self if not our survival.

My last hunt was in the BWCA last year (2018). Phyllis and I were staying at the Gunflint Trail Lodge in a swank cabin because Phyllis could not negotiate the stairs leading to the cabin that we could afford and were originally assigned. Thanks to the staff, we were moved to a cabin that had no steps at no extra charge. The Lodge billed the special rate week as a "Grouse Hunter's Week." I went hunting, although it was hard for me to walk with rheumatism in my knees and the snow was deep. From experience, I know it is difficult to hunt birds on snowshoes – especially if you have to swing to the right for a shot. I actually got a grouse! Lady Phyllis borrowed some flour from the Lodge chef, boiled potatoes and carrots, and, get this – she made grouse gravy for the mashed potatoes. I do not know of another male or female who has ever had or ever made grouse gravy. It is a labor of love. The Ruffed Grouse is a lean bird, so the drippings from a plucked and roasted grouse are meager. Phyllis saved every drop of fat and drippings and made gravy using the carrot water. With homemade bread, it is the most memorable meal that I have ever had, for many reasons. Over eighty years old, I was lucky to get a grouse. The setting with fresh snow and ice across Gunflint Lake all the way across to Canada. Surrounded by Our Father's handiwork and beauty with a meal including grouse gravy! Is there more? I think not. It was a perfect conclusion to a lifetime of hunting. If I never tote a firearm into the fields or woods or marshes again, I will not miss hunting. I am sated.

The evolution of my hunting has been progressing for a number of years now. I now tote a camera into the fields, woods, marshes, and swamps. With a notepad. **Come Autumn**, my legs may not be in the marshes, woods, or uplands, but my heart will be.